DOUBLE VISION

BY JOHN KNOWLES

A Separate Peace

Morning in Antibes

Double Vision

John Knowles

DOUBLE VISION

AMERICAN THOUGHTS ABROAD

The Macmillan Company
New York

"The Road to Jerusalem," "Hussein: Portrait of a King," and "Petra: City of Stone" are reprinted by permission of the publishers of *Holiday*, © The Curtis Publishing Company, 1963. Portions of Part Three and Part Four originally appeared in *Horizon*.

First Printing

Printed in the United States of America

The Macmillan Company, New York
Collier-Macmillan Canada, Ltd., Toronto, Ontario

Library of Congress catalog card number: 64-17600

DESIGNED BY RONALD FARBER

FOR HENRY MCILHENNY

φίλος πολύξενος

CONTENTS

Part

LONDON AND CAMBRIDGE

One

I have never learned a great deal about the countries where I traveled; I haven't even learned a great deal about the countries where I've lived for more or less long periods. Surface things, I've apprehended those: that the Greeks say "Psst!" like conspirators in old spy movies when they want to attract someone's attention; that the English are very talkative people; that Italians are highly conventional; that Arabs often get drunk; that the French don't have much imagination—things like these I have noticed.

But what I did learn a lot about by traveling in other parts of the world was the United States. I always found myself looking at Paris or Beirut or anywhere abroad with bifocal eyes; up close there were the Parisians or the Lebanese behaving as they behaved, and dimly in the distance of my mind's eye there was the American version. What they did abroad was interesting; what we were doing at home was a revelation: I would never have seen it except in that foreign light.

I had no idea this was going to happen through traveling. I believed I already knew the United States very well, and didn't like what I knew very much these days. I had grown tired of useless comfort, I was getting restless in houses so completely furnished and air-conditioned and wired for sound and insulated from the outdoors that the people inside seemed in danger of becoming merchandise too. I have been in too many cars so lavishly sprung that riding in them was like sitting on Jello: I was out of humor with a countryside where driving along you were abruptly confronted by a vast screen occupied by richly colored giants strangely and silently gesturing at each other. The food I ate was uniformly good and always on time, and always the same. I was enjoying the average American privileges; I was sick of them.

My chance to travel came and I seized it, sailing away on a fine old European liner making almost her last crossing. Her name was right for my feelings; she was the *Liberté*.

London. Looking down from the window of my rooms I can see the Westminster Roman Catholic Cathedral up the street. The street is respectable-residential. Behind this apartment is Victoria Station. Nearby are the gardens of Buckingham Palace.

On the street below me there is a lamppost, and next to the lamppost stands a middle-aged man. When one of the infrequent pedestrians passes, the man extends his cap; it is a limp cap and he holds it out in a limp way, limp but not abject, limp but unapologetic, limp but definite. He is not blind and doesn't seem to be crippled in any way. He has just decided to beg, to beg on this unpromising back street: he is not an ambitious beggar. He has not shown the enterprise to dance in the comical, music-hall style two middle-aged men regularly do in the middle of the traffic in Leicester Square; he doesn't sell pencils or keep a performing monkey; he doesn't even choose a likely street. He does only one thing; he lifts that limp cap each time somebody passes. Now and then I have an urge to go down and kick him.

This feeling was my first "American" surge of emotion abroad. As I stood tingling with irritation at the window, looking at the beggar, England for the first time really became foreign to me; this was the kind of beggar "they" had. I also saw in myself for the first time the American disapproval of lassitude, of lack of enterprise, of limpness.

On these overcast June days, the quality of light in London suggested rich old wood; London seemed a narrow, perpendicular city in ripe and rainy colors, mahogany and pearl gray and deep green. This was the "season" and there were parades and regattas and races—often it was sunny—with top hats and shining breastplates and hushed limousines and flowered dresses.

I was invited to quite a few places, and the English, or at least the Londoners, quickly established themselves for me as nonstop talkers, magpies, hurriedly and matter-of-factly unraveling their intimate lives to strangers at parties and in pubs and practically anywhere else. Nothing stopped them. Nor was I expected to be any less frank. "How much do you make a year?" someone would flick out at me after spending ten minutes on his own finances and divorce problems and exactly why the marriage broke up. A very attractive girl I had just met complained on leaving a party about the middle-aged man there who had tried to seduce her again. "Always asking me to go to *Switzerland!*" she said bitterly. A young gentleman launched immediately into a description of his affair with an Italian girl in Trieste and how her fiancé, trying to insult him, had done his best, spitting out at him in a literal translation from Italian, "You unknown, traveling-around-the-world man!" And that is what he had been then and still was, he added. This way of crisply snapping their cards down on the table suggested that they were willing to reveal themselves as irregular in any number of ways, willing to confess and to dare indefinitely, willing to be anything at all except genteel. They seemed to fear that the way New Yorkers feared failure.

I myself am not a New Yorker. Who am I, who is this traveler registering impressions and fears and excitements and prejudices in foreign parts, where does he come from and what is his point of view? Where does he stand himself?

Americans are less and less "regional" these days and I am not, any more. I come from not a town or a city or a region but a segment, the small slice of the United States which begins in northern Virginia and northern West Virginia and moves north, never getting far from the Atlantic Ocean, until it ends in southern New Hampshire and southern Vermont. Its hubs, of course, are New York and Washington. At the time of the Roman Empire, a citizen analogous to me would have lived in the Campagna Romana, Rome and its environs, in and around, that is, the main prop of Western civilization, a spectator and reactor to all the power and pressures at the center. That is who I am and where I live.

In London, at first, the surface pleasures of the Season were the only things open to me. From pub to club to pub to club I went one afternoon with the British author and critic John Davenport, who talked steadily, of course, like all Londoners, but also stimulatingly and intelligently if nearly incomprehensibly in his swift monotone. Somewhere a wild Scottish poet with wild red hair and beard and a wild free tongue joined us and proceeded to drink and quote and drink and recite and drink and improvise all along the way. "Ah, the glory of Scottish poetry!" he cried, and off he waltzed into stanzas of impenetrable verse, eyes sparkling; ah the beauty of it, the truth! If only we others could understand it all! Such a loss for us. Nothing to be done, he couldn't teach us Scottish in an afternoon. Another drink then? Aye.

And out poured more verse and philosophy and affection, spontaneous streams of affection toward John Davenport, toward the barman, toward anyone around, toward me.

His soaring spirits had been making me feel more and more pleased with him and myself and London and life and just as these generous feelings of mine reached their peak he turned a sparkling eye on me and in his edgy, melodious voice said with the greatest pleasure, "Could you let me have five pounds?" and there was something in the timing of this, some instinct he had for the conditioned reflexes of others which propelled my hand into my pocket and produced a five-pound note on the spot. "Let me explain to you exactly where I am staying, so that you can find me," he went on happily, and there followed some swift London directions involving squares and mews and lanes, so swift that I had no time to say that I would rather tell him where I was staying so that *he* could find *me,* but no, no, on went his busy directions, and then with a final cackle and quotation and a shining poet's smile, he rather hurriedly left, leaving me with a strong first impression of Scotland, and of the Scotch.

I continued to ramble around London, admiring so many things about the British—their law, their lawns, their manners, their complexions, their theater, their taxis, their vocabularies, their parliamentary democracy, their leisure. One day I came to their museum—the British Museum—and encountered something that was theirs but had been the Greeks' but that belonged really to everybody. It was a sculptural collection called there the Elgin Marbles, which consists of sculpture taken from the Parthenon in Athens. As I came into the room containing them, the strangeness of Britain, which had been vaguely beclouding me, fell away; these works of art transcended all possible national differences and as I looked at them with wonder, with rapture, I was able to transcend all such differences myself: there were no Britons or Americans or Greeks, or if there were, these superficial categories made no difference: there was Man, he was a miracle, and he was in deadly danger. That was what this sculpture made plain.

The Parthenon metopes were carved in white marble under the supervision of Phidias sometime between 447 B.C. and 432 B.C.; in other words they were work done at the pinnacle of Greek civilization. Pericles, leader of Athens, was undertaking a great temple to the presiding goddess of the city, Athena, and these panels carved in bold relief were part of the decoration of it. They were put in place on the Parthenon above the pillars and below the roof, where they told a continuing story.

They depict a mortal combat between Man and Centaur in fifteen surviving panels, and I have been trying now without success to recall how big they were: none of the books at hand tells; I can't remember. They seemed to fill the vast room and the city. The Centaur rearing forth from the white marble is a brute packed with blunt power in his horse's body and man's torso, arms and head; he is a monster. Against him stands Man, young and well-made but not massive in any way, who must fight the Centaur to the death. The panels depict this seemingly unequal struggle. How can Man prevail against such overwhelming power? He is an evolved, complex being; that can be seen in the carving. There is a violinlike tenuousness about him, he is a higher form of life, one that came into fulfillment only lately. In becoming more complex and evolved Man has had to sacrifice a good deal of plain, blunt force. He has a new resourcefulness now, of course, new intelligence, new—it is plain to see in the carving—nobility present in his character. Can he now sustain himself with these new gifts as a civilized human being despite the brute force he lost in attaining them, in a world still full of brutishness? Imagine the power of such a question in Athens of the time, with mobs of barbarians just beyond the mountains, while in the city achievements we are in awe of today were being made, the great first principles of science and philosophy and art were laid down. That was the question these carvings asked: can Man prevail against the bestiality he himself has struggled out of by a supreme effort? They ask it and very movingly answer it: yes, he can prevail. That is the answer of these sculptured masterpieces, their answer. But the question is still being asked everywhere in the world today, and the answer is not final.

And I thought about America where many of the artists want to throw themselves happily under the hooves of the Centaur, and where the scientists want to wire themselves into electronic machines; and was Man, this vulnerable achievement, going to prevail this time against the current beasts, such as the Bomb, the boredom, and the anti-nature forces of contemporary life?

So, on to death, death in England. Westminster Abbey is a fine, silver-gray English Gothic church built with a sense of stately beauty and dignity. It is overflowing with the dead. As I came through the great north doorway, which is not the main portal but the one to the left of the high altar, there were all the dead, ten, or twenty, or perhaps fifty feet high, Palmerston, Pitt, three versions of Canning (unless there were three Cannings), Disraeli, Gladstone, Peel, all soaring over me in dead white marble. Opposite these political figures there was a vast memorial to Captain William Bayne, Captain William Blair, and Captain Lord Robert Manners. I wondered who they had been. Their monument featured a handsome sculptured woman wearing a helmet, presumably the Goddess of War. Beneath her there was a languid Neptune. Then these captains must have been naval heroes. All right. Behind the Goddess of War there was a lion, presumably representing Britannia. This lion appeared in many other monuments throughout the Abbey and must be described. The best way to do that is in terms of the motion picture *The Wizard of Oz.* The American clown Bert Lahr in that movie played the Cowardly Lion, with ringlets and agonized eyes and a gaping frightened mouth. That is what this lion looks like. Simpering nervously behind the Goddess of War, he held a shield between his two feeble forepaws. Near the bottom of the monument, beneath Neptune, a sea horse was panting under all this load on top of him.

Set into the walls of the Abbey there were many, many other monuments and memorials, and as I looked along the wall I was reminded of reefs seen underseas, encrusted with the accumulation of immobile sea life—coral and clam, shells and seaweed, starfish and barnacles, a rusted beer can, a spent mortar shell, little caves where transparent fish darted, knobs of rock, marine dust, the claw of a lobster, convolutions and promontories of the reef itself—all of it silent as the sea, all of it as still as death. I went on down the nave of the Abbey, past memorial after memorial to nobles and military men and political figures I had never heard of, interspersed at long intervals by a memorial to a British genius everyone had heard of, a glory of Britain who appeared here amid the other dead like a pearl in an oyster bed.

I came on a slab dedicated to Major John André, and far back in my recollection of schoolboy history the name dimly sounded. He had been a British spy, it was during the American Revolution, we had executed him. I couldn't remember what had been notable enough about that to explain its inclusion in grade-school history. The memorial enlightened me a little:

employed in an important but hazardous Enterprise fell a Sacrifice to his Zeal for his King and Country lamented even by his
FOES
His gracious Sovereign King GEORGE the Third
has caused this Monument
to be erected

Above this inscription there was a panel in bold relief showing Major André being led away from his wife, who has averted her head and is wringing her hands. Next to this scene there was another, depicting a messenger delivering a paper to a group of officers, some of them in tears—perhaps these were his lamenting FOES. Above these scenes there was the Goddess of War again, and also the lion, frowning in anguish, his mouth pulled back in suffering and his eyes turned heavenward among his ringlets.

Up the nave, to the left of the main altar I came on one of the biggest monuments of all, and was startled to see that it was dedicated to General Wolfe, the conqueror of Quebec, whose dying words were, of course, among the most famous in English: he said that he would prefer to have written

> The boast of heraldry, the pomp of pow'r,
> And all that beauty, all that wealth e'er gave,
> Await alike the inevitable hour:
> The paths of glory lead but to the grave

than to have taken Quebec.

And here was the grave they gave him, heaped with boasting and power and pomp: this is what they erected over this poet in desire.

First of all there was the siege of Quebec in bronze relief.

Above that there were two lions, wearing unusual expressions. They look like ladies instead of lions, unmarried ladies in their late middle years who have just discovered that their heirloom spoons have been stolen. Above this pair there was a huge sarcophagus. Above that there was Wolfe, nearly naked, very wan, being supported by two of his men. From the upper left an angel is flying down toward his head with a wreath in her hand. And above her it all at last came to a point under what seemed to be from the viewer's position very far below an oriental headdress.

Behind the altar there was the entirely different Edward the Confessor Chapel, containing medieval effigies that represented the rulers of that period, effigies that simply memorialized the illustrious dead. The Throne of England, ancient and battered as the history of England itself, was there resting on the Stone of Scone. And elsewhere there were memorials to Dickens and Handel and Samuel Johnson and Newton and Browning and Darwin and Purcell and so on, lost amid all the noble lords and the politicians who have battened onto the Abbey like coral on a reef, layer after layer of them so that the original church is nearly unrecognizable now and the geniuses of Britain have to be pried out of the crust as if with a trowel.

The egotism and emptiness of much of public life are flaunted there in the cowering old Abbey, and thinking of America it seemed that we had maintained a little more sense in our monuments to dead people. Evelyn Waugh's gorgeous satirical gifts in the novel *The Loved One* showed an Englishman's horror of certain Californian burial habits, but bemused in Westminster Abbey, I wondered why he had traveled so far.

The past might be dead and vulgar, but the present, alive and wise and rich in civilization, beckoned to me: Mr. E. M. Forster invited me to visit him at Cambridge University. In

London I tried to prepare myself, especially psychologically, for this meeting. As it happened I already knew the way. During a short visit to England several years before I had worked up my courage to go and call on Mr. Forster. I knew every line he had published, and so without introduction or any kind of forewarning, I went up to Cambridge and found King's College, where he lived, trailed uncertainly in through the great steepling gate, across the courtyard and up a stairway, up to a large wooden door which had "Mr. Forster" painted on it.

If it had said "Mr. Dickens" I could not have been more shocked. Somehow I was not prepared for that door; I could not reconcile this matter-of-fact sign on it with the novels and stories and biographies and essays which I knew. I thought of the great echo of the Marabar Caves in *A Passage To India* and of the fiery sufferings of *The Longest Journey* and the tough comedy of *Where Angles Fear To Tread,* and the fact of their creator sitting, very probably, behind that wooden door with that sign on it was a little too much for me. I tried to knock but then, impressed with the crudity of myself barging in on this artist in his eightieth year, I brought my hand down, turned and went down the stairs, across the courtyard, through the gate, back to London and home to America.

But now here I was with a letter inviting me to come. In the meantime I had published a novel, *A Separate Peace.* Its reception in England and America, and the letters people wrote to me, were all that any first novelist could have wished, but nothing equalled a letter I got one day written in a rather difficult hand from King's College, Cambridge, comparing something about my book to Sophocles and signed by E. M. Forster.

I took the train from London and it puttered across the subdued countryside under heavy skies. Outside King's College again, I sat down on a low wall and tried to organize myself for the visit, tried to eliminate superficialities and pretensions.

Not at all sure that I had succeeded—I hadn't; can it be done?—I went through the gate, across the courtyard, up the stairs and up to the door. That name on it still seemed hallucinatory to me, but this time I knocked and a cheerful voice called out for me to come in.

The study I entered was large, high-ceilinged and rather dim. My eye noticed a large reproduction of a Picasso painting of a boy leading a horse, and then looking to the left I spied Mr. Forster in a comfortable armchair at the far side of the fireplace. He got up to greet me, a considerably larger man than I had expected, aged certainly, somewhat stooped. He came forward, wearing thin metal-rimmed spectacles on a singularly well-organized face. I had not seen many fully realized faces, but here was one. It looked as if his forebears and his ideas and his character and his life all formed a coherent pattern. It was pointed (the nose), and a little drooping (the light-blue eyes and the gray moustache); it looked as though it had never been good-looking in the conventional sense, and as though what might have been thought weaknesses had been turned into strengths. I thought it showed integrity, sensitivity, and a vast amount of good sense.

He began to fix tea, getting down on all fours before the unlighted fireplace to unplug an electric heater and plug in the pot. There were a great many books in cases along the walls, a long couch, several tables, the originals in light tints of the illustrations used in his *Marianne Thornton,* bits of family memorabilia here and there—"I inherited that from my aunt," he said of a table, "and I shall pass it along in the family when"—an accepting sign—"I die."

I couldn't contain my excitement very well, and began to rattle on about the Algerian rebellion, with which I had had some close to first-hand experience, and why the Algerians inevitably had thrown out the French, one of the reasons for this being, as I badly phrased it, that the Algerian Moslems were "multiplying so fast."

"Multiplying, are they?" he said in a new tone, all benevolence gone, unemphatically but definitely challenging. He didn't like at all what sounded like condescension in me toward another race. I heard that and quickly explained what I thought and felt and knew about Algerians, and there was peace between us again.

There is something deeply sincere in the finest writers, a deeply sincere, profound sense of the importance of life. It's not a quality much admired today among people who are in the lead and in the know and up on everything, and it is often concealed behind an exterior alive with paradox and indifference and superiority, but it always seems to be there. In Ernest Hemingway it expressed itself in his shyness, in Thornton Wilder in a glittering but purposeful, responsible loquacity, in William Faulkner in an exquisite muteness. In Mr. Forster it appeared in the most impressive form of all: he seemed ready to revise his ideas, carved out during a long, distinguished and authoritative lifetime, if something I said seemed to make this necessary. If he honored me this way then he must honor practically everyone. He was experimenting still, experimenting in his eighties, still weighing and testing life, strong but not rigid in his views, growing; he hadn't given up the struggle out of fatigue or boredom and done the easier thing of burying doubt and effort under his laurels. I found him listening closely as I rambled on about the Moslems, the French, America.

Finally getting control of my elation, I gave him an opportunity to speak.

He told me that he was leaving for Italy in a few days: in his novels the characters are always leaving for Italy, where a few of them are saved from the curse of Anglo-Saxonism. His characters traveled by train and carriage: Mr. Forster was taking a jet. It was a measure of the changes that had occurred during his adult life: they have been so radical that they silenced him, as a creator of fiction, thirty years ago. Much of modern life he did not find up to his standards; for example, there is no "fineness," he said, in the motion picture, and so "I won't let them get at my stuff," thereby sacrificing a fortune. I pointed out to him that someday his copyrights will expire and then his work will be at the mercy of everybody, and suggested it might be better to let it be filmed while he could in some measure control it. No, no, it was true that someday the novels would be in the public domain, but "I shall not be here to see it."

Flying, on the other hand, was something he liked, had never had any fear of—"I don't have that kind of imagination"—but he had liked it best before it consisted in being rocketed in a capsule thirty or forty thousand feet above the ground. He recalled flying over France in a little plane, with the beautiful French countryside spreading on all sides a few hundred feet below him, and as the sun began to set the rivers and streams of France were fired up in its long rays "like the veining of a leaf."

And then he turned his attention to me, and what I should do. Apparently Mr. Forster had noticed that I was one of the live-around-the-world types the British themselves produced in abundance.

He sensed that, and he was right. I had been the type of boy who, at the age of twelve, would slowly turn the globe of the world until I saw a name perhaps in the lower Malay States, and then think to myself, "It must be wonderful to live there"; or maybe some solitary settlement near the Arctic Circle would enchant me by its solitude, or a spur of land in Central America, or some island off East Africa, or a corner of the Balkans—"Zagreb," I would murmur in awe to myself,

"Zagreb"—or a town on the Upper Nile, far, far up the Upper Nile. I simply couldn't make up my mind which of these wonderful places would be the place to live, and at twelve I realized with a wave of disappointment that even the huge amount of life stretching ahead of me probably would not be long enough to fulfill what really underlay this fascination with place: a wish to live everywhere in the world.

In listening to my earlier flood of talk, Mr. Forster had realized he had one of these characters before him. Also, he had read my book and so knew many other things about me.

"Why don't you go to Greece on one of these trips of yours?" he remarked.

Greece? I made the excuse that I wouldn't be able to say a word to anybody there. I was on my way now to Lebanon where they spoke French, and to Jordan, where many people spoke English. Greece?

"Greece is a wonderful country," he said unemphatically. "It's the people. . . ." And he let it go at that—indicated his advice and let it go at that. Mr. Forster has never shouted his beliefs, which is one reason people in the end have listened so intently to them.

But it took me a long time to listen to this advice; not for the first time in my life, I sailed stubbornly past a pointer that was meant for me.

Not even E. M. Forster could persuade me to go to Greece. I had a clear picture in my mind of what Greece was like, a picture formed from half-read newspaper stories, passing remarks by people who had changed planes in Athens, and I don't very clearly remember what else. But I was certain the picture was accurate, and so Greece was one of the few countries in the world I didn't want to see. First of all, there was nothing in Greece except Athens. All the rest was inhabited by a sprinkling of depressed peasants and fishermen. Athens was strewn around the Acropolis, which, while beautiful and inspiring, only accentuated the dreariness of the contemporary city. The city was a cluttered, dirty, grim little assemblage of cafés where gloomy men in black suits talked interminably over their coffee about politics. There were only men to be seen; visitors were never allowed to see Greek women. The food could not be eaten by the non-Greek, nor could he survive the summer heat. There were no hotel rooms to be rented, but only beds in a room with seven or eight other beds occupied by strange and probably sinister people.

All of this, my historical sense told me, was because the barbarians had overrun classical Greece and destroyed not only the civilization and the economy but the very soul of the people by intermarrying with them, drowning the beauty and nobility of the Greeks in a sea of barbarian blood. Nobody was there today except stunted, ugly, stupid descendants of the barbarian hordes, talking, talking over their handlebar moustaches about politics. It was the last place I wanted to visit.

Mr. Forster did not repeat his advice or give his reasons beyond "It's the people . . ." because I had not shown enough interest, and after tea we got up, he put on a long overcoat and a floppy tweed cap, and we went out across the beautiful college lawn on which only Fellows of the college and their guests may walk, into the famous chapel with its great English Gothic nave, the altar screen, ribbed ceiling, stylized windows—most of all with its smell of candle wax and candle smoke and ancient leather and wood polish—and then out of the college to the taxi. This would take me to the train to London and the train to Venice and the ship to the Near Orient and finally the horse into Petra and the night in the cave, and at the taxi stand I said good-bye, got into the cab, and as it pulled away I turned to wave once more through the oval back window, and my last glimpse of the greatest living English novelist was of a tall old man in a long billowing overcoat gaily and energetically waving his cap after me.

In my last days in London I was once again carried along the fringes of the Season, and the London candor struck me with new force. How emancipated these people were, regular children of nature! England's supposed prudery and coldness and hypocrisy and reserve must all be dead then, the liberation of the English spirit worked for by Mr. Forster and D. H. Lawrence and others must have been achieved.

Even the fringe of the Season can tire you out after a while, and one afternoon at about five o'clock I found time for a nap. I undressed to my shorts and lay down. The one long window in the bedroom was letting in quite a bit of light through its white muslin curtain so I got up, went to the window, pulled the draperies shut and lay down again. Perhaps half an hour later the doorbell rang. I got up, put on bathrobe and slippers, and went to the door. Two tall bobbies were there.

"Are you the occupant of this flat?" one of them asked politely.

"Yes."

After an indeterminate, curious pause he continued, with a trace of pleasant confusion, "May we—do you mind—?" gesturing toward the inside.

"Come in," I said. This must be some civil-defense check, I thought, or perhaps there is a gas leak.

They came into the hall.

"Lead on," the spokesman for the two said.

I indicated the living room, but they hesitated, orienting themselves, and then headed for the bedroom. I followed in gathering puzzlement.

The spokesman crossed to the window, opened the draperies briefly, and then turned to me and said politely enough, "Would you mind telling us, sir, what you were doing this afternoon?"

"Taking a nap just now. Could you tell me—?"

"Did you sleep?"

"No. Why are—?"

"Did you at any time come to the window here?"

"I closed the draperies, yes. I'm sorry, but you're going to have to tell me what this is all about."

There was a short pause and then he said, "There is a lady across the street who says you were exposing yourself indecently at the window."

The boat train for the Continent left Victoria Station at two in the afternoon.

In my compartment there was the usual loquacious Englishman sitting across from me who tried to start a conversation, but I had had enough of the English and their confidences and retreated behind my newspaper until he stopped. The sedate countryside moved past the window, and I looked at it with the squint of a foreigner, with real beady-eyed mistrust. What was finally behind the apparently open, candid face of England? What did they really have lurking at the bottom of those gardens? Wasn't there the worm of hypocrisy gnawing ceaselessly away? Weren't the various "daring" self-revelations English acquaintances had treated me to only the reverse side of the woman in the building across the way? Weren't the English, now and always, laced up with guilt, muddled with self-deceptions about sex?

The woman across the way was the most transparent case at hand. In thinking about her I wondered how, unless she had the vision of an eagle or else raked my building regularly with binoculars, she could have seen me at all. My bedroom was at the end of a deep, dark inset; there was the white muslin curtain which she had to penetrate, there was a very wide street between her building and mine.

I had, as a matter of fact, not noticed her building at all. I investigated later, and saw that it was a business building. So there she must have been, sitting at her desk, her eyes at every free moment roaming back and forth over the dozens of windows visible across the street from her, thinking to herself that it was just idle curiosity, just something to do, all the while combing the street for an outlet for her need to see the sex she felt was somewhere all around her, yet gallingly invisible. And then she spotted me: a shape, male; he's naked, her needs told her, and he's doing something indecent. That is what she wanted to see, so that's what she saw. But at this point we move away from her psychological problems into a wider social context. At this moment, by the slightest muscular effort, she could have shifted her gaze dozens of yards away. Why hadn't she done that? Or she could have done what a Frenchwoman sitting next to me at a movie newsreel did when the screen suddenly showed naked coalminers taking showers, and burst out laughing. No. Her training was different. She called the police. And they undertook to enforce her will and support her with the full force of the law.

Well, that apparently was what was done in England, just as though nothing had ever been discovered by the classical Greeks, by Shakespeare, by Freud, about the unconscious mind, just as though Britain were still living in some kind of savage ignorance, in a stupidity where lies about human nature are enforced by law.

The widespread contempt for law among youth today is partly a result of this. Youth expects and respects realism and fairness in adults, and the spectacle of the law enforcing an out-of-date "morality" any alert sixteen-year-old could see through disgusts them.

The woman across the way was a grim little reminder of

self-ignorance, and the wrongness of righteousness, and of how far behind the understanding of the times the law always is.

And thinking about America, I knew that we were no better.

Still, there was no defense like innocence, and by the time the bobby told me what I had been accused of he must have been almost certain that he had made a mistake. When I opened the door and saw those two large policemen standing there, I had simply said, "Yes?" calmly, and not looked at all scared. I had willingly let them in. And when they did at last tell me why they were there, my lack of guilt was proved conclusively.

That is, I exploded. But here the peculiar poison of false accusation began to seep through. I knew that my anger was establishing my innocence, and I began to act even angrier than I was. And what if my acting began to ring false? The ice was beginning to thin dangerously: how good an actor *was* I? I began, in other words, to experience the emotions of guilt; that's what a false accusation can do to you.

". . . and who is this frustrated old woman accusing . . . accusing me, what kind of a country is this!"

"Would you care to give us your name? You don't have to."

I blurted out my name and much other information, including how outraged I was and so on, and after a while the bobby had had enough of me and my outrage.

"You realize, sir, that on the basis of this lady's statement we could take you along and file charges against you."

I felt a wave of fear at that. Up in my mind rose visions of my name in the London newspapers which specialize in sex stories, transatlantic phone calls to relatives, to . . . to somebody or other, and their thin, baffled voices betraying the suspicion that I must have done *something* to get into such a mess, most of all a far-away-from-homeness feeling swept over me, and also an aversion for the particular nature of the charge itself, the thin unpleasantness of "indecent exposure" as opposed, for example, to the straightforward boldness of rape: all of this crashed down on me and I clamped my mouth shut.

That was all the bobby wanted; a decent show of respect for the law in me. But once again I was acting, successfully; I had no respect for their law now. Now I was almost blindly angry but with just enough sense left to realize that anything more said, no matter how justified, would only prolong the peculiar, tricky peril a disturbed woman's imagination had placed me in.

After an impressive silence, they left—I will never forget the silent one's cheery "Cheerio!" as he went out the door—and scared and furious, I began to pack, as I had planned to do anyway, to pack for the boat train, the next stage on the long trek to the desert. "I like the desert," Lawrence of Arabia, the most notable fugitive from the sex complexes of England, was supposed to have said, "because it's clean."

At Folkstone the train pulled in beside the Channel boat, and in Sicilian confusion we transferred to it. Somewhere in the confusion I lost my passport case containing my passport, several hundred dollars, and other valuable things. I settled onto the deck of the ship, unaware of any loss, thankful that my experience of Britain was ended. But it wasn't quite. Just before we sailed a minor dock official came up to me and politely returned my passport case, which still contained my passport, several hundred dollars, and everything else.

Part

PARIS
VENICE
BEIRUT

Two

The French train slid across Normandy. I had a compartment to myself, spacious and rich with vintage comfort, with polished wood, carpet, even a little radiator in the corner. The window was open, and summertime Normandy smelled wonderfully grassy and productive, fresh and fertile and rich and optimistic. During the afternoon I got into conversation with a thin young Italian who might have been a gondolier or a tenor but who happened to be a representative for Vicks VapoRub, in Florence. We arrived at the Gare du Nord after dark: *"Parigi!"* he cried in delight, grinning widely at the Sacré-Cœur basilica, its white turrets gleaming in the night. The train rolled on to the Gare de Lyon for a two-hour halt before heading for the Alps. It was the depth of summer, and every Parisian who could afford to had left the city. The great railroad station snoozed in a dusty tranquillity, slept and dreamed in a still, late-evening trance; ambling along the platform in a reverie came a railroad man who stopped to philosophize with me about travel, and weather, and life; a cart with soft drinks stood unattended nearby, but then nobody needed service; the vague lights blurred in this vast steel cave, voices carried far but had little to say and lots of time to say it; the slow, thoughtful peace of Paris in the summer slumbered over the Gare de Lyon. The Vicks Italian wanted to glimpse Paris, of course, but at the same time he was afraid of it, perhaps because of its sins, so like a Guardian Angel I went along with him as he ventured into a café across from the station for a cup of coffee, and then on foot around one or two blocks; that was as much as he wanted to risk, and we roamed through the empty streets under a light drizzle back to the brooding and philosophical station.

On our train there were cars marked "Lausanne" and "Brig" and "Milan" and "Trieste," a train waiting for mystery and intrigue and spies, its cars a dark dashing green on the outside, stuffed comfort within, poised now in the hub of Europe's railroading where at this one brief period of the year there was silence, while along the lines radiating in all directions crowds hurried aboard, jammed corridors and stepped on one another, screamed and spent, slept wretchedly and dropped orange peels on the floor and snapped at the children and worried and hurried and finally staggered off the noisy monster at whatever temporarily jammed corner of France they had chosen as an escape from the frantic life of Paris.

The train slowly and it seemed reluctantly drew out of the dreaming city, heading east. I was spending no more time than that in France. I looked on France the way a man looks on his wife after an amicable divorce: what a fine woman she is, how many admirable qualities; thank God I'm rid of her. Or perhaps I can put it this way: in spite of everything, some of my best friends are French. I'm moderation itself on this subject compared to virtually every American between the ages of twenty and forty who has talked about France with me. Most of them flush at the mention of the name of the country and then begin to use foul language; surely no country in the world rivals France as an object of young American loathing. They are mystified by the "lost" generation, which, following the First World War was magnetized by Paris and France, huddling there in the glow of the culture, the charm, the art, the adventure, the civilization they thought they found among the French. The present generation of young American writers will go almost anywhere else; one of them, Truman Capote, has gone hundreds of miles out of his way to avoid setting foot in Paris; others hurry tight-lipped through it and on to anywhere at all, as long as it is not French. This is not just because Paris has become one of the most expensive cities in the world; it's a revulsion they feel against the Parisian personality, a cold disdainfulness they find there. They have heard too many Parisians saying in their high, flat voices (female) or surly growls (male), "No, that cannot be done, no, that is impossible, no, there is an extra charge for that, no, that cannot be arranged, no, we have no such provisions, no, your bill is accurate, there is a charge for, and a charge for, and a charge for, no, I cannot discuss the weather with you, no, I have never thought of going to America, or to England, no, I do not read about other countries, no, you cannot sit there, no, I cannot understand a word of your French, no, there is no ticket out of Paris available, no, you cannot walk to the frontier, there is a regulation against that."

One reason for their churlishness is that the French, and particularly the Parisians, are tired of us; they're weary of hearing American voices, they're fed up with seeing and disliking American clothes, they are so irritated by what Americans do to their language that they decline to understand them, they want to be left to themselves, tourist money —no American will believe this part—isn't finally that important to them.

Their disinclination to like postwar Americans was tremendously increased by the French postwar inferiority complex. Their collapse in 1940 was a huge shock. Whatever General de Gaulle said, they really had lost a war, and it was Britain, the United States and the Soviet Union which removed the consequences of that defeat from them. Then followed the drawn-out, agonizing humiliation of losing their Empire, piece by bloody piece. The French were used to thinking of themselves, in a quietly well-mannered way, as the best people in the world, and enduring this wretched procession of humiliations soured them toward themselves first and then toward successful foreigners, especially those who had saved them.

The French do not have the best dispositions in the world under any circumstances, and in their twenty-year ordeal following 1940 the circumstances were always awful. They had never been given to quick enthusiasms, to spontaneous affections, or to admire simplicity; they had been educated to analyze, to discriminate, to value *la mesure*—the just proportion—and in the late 'forties they began to find their oracular Paris overflowing with these bouncing victors from America, all sincere, all seemingly monied in underpaid France, all simple, all, it seemed to them, inferior to Parisians in most categories. Meanwhile the United States was saving their economy with the Marshall Plan. It was too much to be borne by people as proud as the French.

Finally, in 1958, 1959 and 1960, I watched this inferiority complex dissolve as General de Gaulle removed one plaguing problem after another. A stable franc was established, so was a stable government; above all, the terrible sense that the country was always sliding, in the value of its money and the makeup of the government and the size of the Empire, that sense of sliding was at last halted. The albatross of Algeria was cut loose, and the countries of Europe rushed to join themselves with France in a Common Market just as vehemently as the Imperial pieces had rushed from her. France found her role and got into step with time at last. Prosperity erupted; they began paying back in advance the huge loans we had granted them; it became just conceivable that we might some day have to ask them for a loan. They began to like us a little.

But I still didn't want to go there, for the final reason that, I think, it doesn't suit traveling young Americans at all. When you are young you travel in order to see wonders, to be excited, stimulated, for adventure. The place for this following the Second World War, everyone for some mysterious reason supposed, was France. But except for riots and murders resulting from the Algerian revolution, there was little of it to be had there. France was and is one of the least exciting, in that sense, or adventurous countries in the world. The young American, fooled by the novelty of the language and the food and this and that surface feature, imagined that soon the real excitement, the real adventure of being abroad would begin. It never did. France remained profoundly bourgeois, tightly clamped in its centralized Napoleonic order, organized down to the last metal chair, which you have to pay to sit on, in the smallest park. It was a place for orderly people to live, it existed for them; visitors simply clogged up the machinery. The inhabitants were gifted and cautious and not at all outgoing. Everything has been done to make life calm and orderly, regulated and limited and inward-looking. Left hanging around out in the cold, the young American headed for the frontier, scornful of France without knowing why, not realizing that he had gone to the Sahara to look for trees.

I fell asleep on the outskirts of Paris and woke up the next morning as we were pulling into a town called Sion, Switzerland, having slept past Lausanne and Lake Geneva. The train glided easily on, up a steep-walled and narrow valley. The sullen skies of London and the drizzle of Paris had given way to plain Swiss rain. A smoky green stream swung down the middle of the valley, which was an orderly, happy-looking, very green place, with mountains suddenly rearing up from the valley floor. During the night the train had become extremely Swiss and efficient; it hurried uneventfully in a few hours across Switzerland and into the Simplon Tunnel.

The Simplon Tunnel is twelve miles long, long for a tunnel, unbelievably short considering the difference in the worlds it connects. After a long hurtle through the blackness of the tunnel there was an abrupt opening; the train shot out into a weird tiny steep canyon with a stony village dewy under sudden sunshine; then back into blackness and then out again into a narrow valley. I opened the big compartment window and a wave of sun power hit me suddenly and strongly; the train's whistle echoed cheerfully down the steep valley, and behind us the gloomy clouds of the North had been caught and held by the last Alps; the shifting, moody weather of the North was trapped behind them, and an immobile spaceless blue Mediterranean sky spread endlessly overhead. Flowers and trees crowded around. *"Italia!"* cried the Vicks man with a shining smile. A cloud of pine smell came through the open window, and then a smell of greenness of all kinds; we passed a small and beautiful blue lake on the left, and then a much larger lake—Maggiore—very blue under the sun, with a crowd of orange roofs on its far shore and mountains rising squarely and symmetrically, as though placed by hand, behind the town; *"Italia* is the garden of Europe!" said the Florentine, all his defenses falling away; he was safe again under the mantle of Holy Mother the Church. Houses accumulated along the right-of-way, and power lines began to compete with the cypresses for dominance on the skyline; we came tearing down out of the mountain simplicity into bustling North Italy, into Milan, where I boarded another train going east. Soon in the afternoon sunshine the plains of Lombardy were going by in an unrivaled lushness, a splendor of fertility, every square inch of soil producing its maximum. In the late afternoon the train went shrieking over a very long causeway and at the end of it arrived at the rickety lace city of Venice.

In London I had spent an hour with Lieutenant General Sir John Bagot Glubb, the famous Glubb Pasha of the Arab Legion, who had passed his life among the Arabs of the Near East, where he developed a particular intimacy and a relationship of mutual respect with many. "They are the closest people in the world to us, you know," he remarked. Were they? If by "us" he meant the whole European-American Western-culture peoples, he must be right, although to me they seemed as remote as Venutians. I had decided to spend some time among them myself, to go over the rim of Western culture and into the world of Islam, and stay until I got the staleness of America out of my system.

I met one other famous person at that time, a young Frenchman who was the leader in his field of applied art, and told him where I was going. "You're going to be bored," he said quietly, "bored. . . ."

The Greek liner *Agamemnon* was due to sail from Venice for Beirut at two the next afternoon. I left my hotel at the Lido in what seemed plenty of time for both of us to get there. I wasn't traveling alone: I had ninety pounds of baggage. During the next months I was going to live in climates ranging from the unthinkable heat of the Dead Sea Valley to the blizzards of the Anti-Lebanon, which meant bringing every piece of clothing I had; and then there were the books: *Jordan* by Ann Dearden, George Kirk's *A Short History of the Middle East from the Rise of Islam to Modern Times,* Hitti's *History of the Arabs,* Lawrence's *The Seven Pillars of Wisdom,* Glubb's *A Soldier with the Arabs, Hussein of Jordan* by Gerald Sparrow, Morris's *The Hashemite Kings,* and so on and so on. I and the ninety pounds reached the dock at the Lido. The *Agamemnon* was several miles away across open water. There was a sleek motorboat for hire there, but it was reserved. Could another one be sent for? The man at the dock telephoned. No, there was no other one available. Well then, what was I supposed to do? I had to get to that ship. Swim for it, holding the bags in my teeth?

But *signore* realizes there is the water-bus, which will be here in a few minutes. He can take that across the Lagoon and down the Grand Canal, disembark at the stop called Accademia, and from there a porter can carry his luggage to the ship in a few minutes, a ten-minute walk at the most.

A ten-minute walk in the rain: a first-class thunderstorm was rolling with lots of electricity up the Adriatic toward us.

Rain? No, *signore,* it never rains in Venice in the summer. Never.

The water-bus arrived, and I and my ninety pounds of baggage were loaded aboard. Two hundred other passengers also piled in, approximately twice capacity, and packed like deportees en route to extermination we started uncertainly across the Lagoon toward the Grand Canal. The storm then broke over the boat in heavy flailing curtains.

At St. Mark's Square I waited for them all to get off. Instead, with great hesitation, two or three passengers persuaded themselves to disembark, one of them falling heavily as he set foot on the dock, then about twelve people got on board. The water-bus backed doubtfully off, and then rolled slowly on down the deserted canal in the downpour.

I couldn't see the name of the next stop through the fogged window, and by the time I was able to struggle over to the window and clear it we were pulling off again. I saw the sign: Accademia.

Damn! Couldn't anything go right in Italy? Pushing my way, not at all gently, against the pressing crowd, I shouted and at the same time tried to drag my ninety pounds of baggage along with me.

Bright dark eyes, bright olive faces, veils, dangling cigarettes and berets turned to focus inquiringly at me. Then they understood; that was all that was necessary. A young girl tried to lift my thirty-five pound suitcase for me. A mother hoisted the other one forward with surprising strength. The rest of my luggage followed the same way, and I myself was passed along from hands to hands, and all was cheerfully unloaded at the next stop.

The water-bus left. I was on a small covered dock, and there was a young officer there standing behind a small high desk and wearing an officer's cap, and that was all there was. My ship was half a mile away, across numerous canals, and there was no boat of any kind. The Grand Canal was completely deserted; it was still raining. I began explaining my predicament to him in handfuls of bungled Italian, and he listened with interest and a smile of some kind slowly widening on his face. No, there was no boat here, no telephone, no recourse, nothing to be done. He continued to smile, which did not improve my disposition. I fell bitterly silent. Time was running out; it was becoming clear: I was going to miss the boat.

And then a gondola glided slowly into view on the empty canal, a black and pointed and leaning and ornate gondola. I shouted, and the gondola, with one oarsman fore and one aft, slowly wheeled in the choppy green water of the canal and headed toward me. Explanations were yelled back and forth as they got closer; they pulled alongside, took the canvas cover off the seat, and handed me and my baggage in. The man on the dock was just as smiling and unsurprised by this outcome as he would have been by the other; I decided he cast some small additional light on the problem of the Mona Lisa. Then, as I was being rowed across the Grand Canal with the steady, limited, successful force of human power itself, the rain stopped; we slid through a network of little back canals, emerging finally into the vast Canale della Giudecca, there was a high white liner, the *Agamemnon,* at the wharf, and we slowly pulled up to her in the bright Italian sunshine.

The *Agamemnon* entered the Gulf of Corinth. Agamemnon—Helen—Clytemnestra—Orestes—Mycenae. I was beginning to get very far away—very, very far away. The last belch from America had expired on the outer edge of the Venice Lagoon, and moving through the still, sun-heavy Adriatic, I was now definitely gone. It was a refreshing feeling, somehow a sweet feeling, like a return to very early youth; there was a sense of morning, and even of innocence about it. That was what travel did for me, but only in the further reaches of abroad, where the groove had not been deeply worn in advance by everyone from Benjamin Franklin and Henry James to Zelda Fitzgerald and Elizabeth Taylor, where the guideposts were few and ambiguous, and the accommodations simple or nonexistent, where they didn't know quite what to make of me and I didn't know what to make of them, where I had to improvise in a new and unfamiliar world; in other words, to behave like someone very young.

The Greek mainland, jagged, spare and empty, rose in a bluish mist on the left, the Peloponnesus, looking the same, was on the right, and as we slid on they converged, drawing closer and closer until they met, and right there had been cut a corridor, a hallway of blue water going straight between two very high steep walls of rock, and reduced now to a stately rate of speed the *Agamemnon* moved into the canal in the stillness and the overpowering sunshine of the Greek noon; the ash-colored walls loomed higher and higher and then declined again, and the ship moved majestically out of the Corinth Canal into a vast, blazing and empty universe of sea—the Aegean itself—and that was the end of Europe; everything ahead was to be oriental.

Nobody had ever told me that fact and I had not gathered it from my mountain of books. Where I was going was called "the Middle East," or sometimes "the Near East," or "the Levant," or "the Arab world," or "Islam." But what it should be called to prepare you for it is "the Orient," and the people "Asiatic Orientals."

Beirut. Looking down from the window of my room I can see a ten- or eleven-year-old boy shooting birds with a rifle. This section is respectable-residential. It overlooks the Mediterranean and is called one thing by the English-speaking, another by the French, and a third by the Arabs. Near the boy there is a hovel of tin and cardboard and rags. Several—I couldn't figure out exactly how many—people lived in it. Other apartment houses, all of them glassily modern, are scattered at complete random over the hillside behind, and so are other hovels. Occasionally garbage flashes by my small balcony into a pit below. One night there was a good deal of gunfire not far away. Sometimes drums beat hypnotizingly for hours in the night. The outside wall of this little apartment is entirely glass, and one night I started to undress and forgot to close the curtains, and then with a start the London business came back to me, and I headed immediately for the curtains. But through the window the lights of Beirut winked in the satiny Levantine blackness, and, remembering where I was, I burst out laughing. "Indecent exposure," in Lebanon: in the murk and fumes of Asia the preposterousness of the charge was clear. Women here blocked undesired sights with their veils, and it seemed unlikely that there was any Lebanese man so sexually timid that exposing himself publicly constituted any particular pleasure, or that there was any Lebanese women with such muddled values that she would cry "Indecent!" at the sight of a male body, or that if she did the Lebanese police would know what in the world she was trying to complain about. That kind of thinking existed on the other side of the Corinth Canal, back there in Britain, and back home in America, back there where all the progress was and where all the sex conflicts were, and where society and the laws passively mirrored those conflicts.

Not that Lebanon was the Elysian Fields, although I thought so at first, as the *Agamemnon* approached it in the morning across the endless, sun-suffused Mediterranean. As the Republic of Lebanon came closer in the clear morning light I saw that the country formed a natural theater: the sea was the stage, the coastal plain, stuffed with fertility and extending only a few miles inland, was the orchestra, and behind rose the galleries—tier on tier of hills going up into great mountains, and on up to peanut heaven, buried in snow. Standing anywhere in Lebanon I had the impression that I could see practically everyone else in the country—it's only thirty-five miles wide, and a hundred and twenty miles long—because as in all good theaters, the sight lines were clear. I felt that no isolation or even privacy was possible; with a good telescope it would seem possible to find out everything about everybody. Beautiful, I said to myself as the *Agamemnon* drew nearer and nearer, what a beautiful country. Everyone who lives here must be beautiful, I thought to myself, and everyone must be good.

The Lebanese don't drive cars; they fire them like guns. A flying phalanx of cars came careening at me down a Beirut street, rattling, screeching, like a really tough American stock-car race; there were only two or three stoplights in the city; at other crossings you picked a lull in the hurtling waves of steel and ran for it. There were no buses. Public transportation consisted of streetcars, almost always extremely overloaded, and a rattletrap fleet of Mercedes-Benzes which covered the city in an unreliable grid pattern and were called the "Service," pronounced in the French way. You did not have to hail them: a driver was constantly hailing you, and if your destination was more or less in his direction he would take you there, picking up and dropping other passengers along the way, usually for half a Lebanese pound—fourteen cents. During my first days, as people in these unmarked Mercedes-Benzes kept calling out to me, I thought this was the world's friendliest city where everybody gave everybody else a lift. Taking a private taxi was difficult because the names of few streets in Beirut meant anything; you had to know instead the name of the section of the city you were going to—not the English or the French but the Arabic word for it—and once there you had to stop and inquire at as many cafés as necessary until you found your destination. A few buildings were famous enough to be known to your driver, and so were a few people. For the rest, you fumbled. Moving around Beirut was hurtling, slapdash, haphazard, inexpensive, inefficient, adventurous, and nerve-racking.

So was driving yourself. One day in an American friend's car I drove down a one-way street the wrong way. At the bottom of it a policeman in khaki uniform and piked pith helmet stopped me. He was young and tall and mustached. We discovered French. I had broken an important Lebanese traffic regulation, he informed me. Could he see the car's registration? I looked for it and couldn't find it. Did the car belong to me? No, it was a friend's. Then perhaps I could show him my driver's license. I did have that, a West Virginia driver's license, and showed it to him. But this license was not good in Lebanon, not good at all. Only an international driver's license was valid here. I was surprised to hear it, because I had driven in Europe with this license and it had been valid there. Ah yes, he replied triumphantly, but this was the East! He then proceeded to prove that by waving me on.

This was the East. A profound carelessness pervaded the life of Beirut, an empirical, striated disorder and randomness. If you didn't want something, out the window with it! If you were putting up a building, put it there, anywhere, anyway, and if you ran out of money for it or lost control of it to your enemy halfway built, never mind. Forget it. Do you want to catch a lot of fish in front of your house? Bomb the water. Does the movie bore or offend you? Riot. It was not the films but the audiences in Beirut which were orchestrated—groaning, sighing, screaming, sweeping from emotion to emotion in perfect synchronization with the plot.

These creatures of passion seemed unrelated to the land they lived on. I had half expected people like the Swiss to inhabit this exhilarating slice of mountain and sea, people sober and bright-faced and simple, leading calm lives among these rangy mountains spreading spaciously down almost to the long straight blue line of the Mediterranean, the mountainsides speckled and knotted with arbors and orchards and groves of trees, with strips and knobs of rock showing through; there was a wholesomeness about the countryside and a small-big look, neat but rangy, all of it most of the time bathed and sparkling under a perfect, domed Mediterranean sky. It seemed a countryside for people who were calm, orderly and sober—which, however, was just what the Lebanese were not.

Does a land create a people? Do the climate and the water and what can be grown there mold them, force them to be a certain kind of people? Were the classical Greeks, for instance, an accident of geography, generated because of a rare, a unique combination of sea and soil and wine and crops which prevailed there for a while, shafts from their environment acting on them like the bombardments of the nucleus of the atom which at a final point of intensity causes a chain reaction?

The Lebanese flatly contradicted this theory, but then their land had always been a portal to Asia, an anteroom and a corridor, too busy, too much coming and going on it for a coherent crop of people to be raised.

And America? I began to remember the natural splendor of our country, the Hudson Palisades, the Grand Tetons, the smoky, rounded beauty of the Alleghenies, the lovely flow of the Shenandoah Valley, and then I thought of the bleak, man-made face we have set down on it, the thousands of fake-brick storefronts, the roadside shambles of snack bars and mattress salesrooms and foam rubber centers and miniature golf courses, the stark downtowns of the small towns, the prettifying which passes for beauty in the homes of the affluent, the sad ugliness of it all, as though there were something unmanly and un-American about making anything beautiful in any way, or just anything that looked nice even, a Protestant punishing rejection of beauty. Wasn't the reason for this that we are not native to the American soil at all, and that's why there is such a contradiction between it and us? What the land itself produced was the American Indian, whose life of strenuous simplicity rose naturally out of the country. And here was the representative American today, predominantly Protestant, predominantly North European, predominantly mercantile, predominantly middle-class, perched uneasily on the usurped soil. North America is the only place in history where a land of such vastness was seized and held permanently by invaders who did not even intermarry but succeeded in virtually wiping out the native race. Therefore the American experience is unique, and the American sense of isolation sharp and understandable. The Negroes naturally felt this most strongly and expressed it most directly: "Sometimes I feel like a motherless child a long way from home." That is a very American feeling.

Sometimes it seems the American people would really be happier if our country were all like Belgium: crowded, monochrome, under continual lowering skies.

It undoubtedly took the Indians, originally immigrants from Asia, many centuries to become americanized, and the process has begun with us, in a deeply unsettling way. The slow action of the land on us helps explain, perhaps explains entirely, why the American character is unintegrated, unresolved, a careful Protestant with a savage stirring in his insides, a germ of native American wildness thickening in his throat.

This wild native strain may have been absorbed by us from the look of our leaves in the autumn, and the smell of them burning, and the smell of American wood burning, and the taste of our corn and turkey, and from our tobacco, and from the wind, and the slant of the American sun.

That may have caused the violent streak in our national life, which the British find so surprising in a country they spawned, just as a New Yorker will be dumbfounded, coming from his city where the police kill and are killed with great regularity, to discover that the London police are not even armed. Everyone is aware of the absorption in violence and sadism of a wide American public, notably including the children and adolescents. Then there are the astonishing number of Americans who commit crimes with no goal or profit in view, strictly for the experience, and usually aware that this is their only real motive. American life has an orderly, rather dull and sober surface, but with something berserk stirring in its depths.

The Lebanese seemed similarly unrelated to their healthful, optimistic-looking land, aliens like us, and with similar dangerous depths. It was by living among them that I saw that in us.

Sitting on a stone bench overlooking the Mediterranean late one afternoon I began to feel a little chilly from an unseasonal wind sweeping along the seafront, carrying the usual dirty paper and grape skins and other refuse along with it. A young Arab came along aimlessly and sat down on the bench near me. He was wearing a white Asiatic cloth coat, not unlike a doctor's smock in the West. He spoke a little English, and we began to talk haltingly. He had been born in Palestine, and fled from it as a small boy during the war of 1948–1949. With his parents, I guessed. No, they were dead, killed in the war. Both? Both of them. He was an extremely quiet kind of person and the expression on his face was gentle but dazed, dazed it seemed permanently, living in a continual state of shock. He inhabited one of the mud and tin shanty towns scattered around Lebanon and Jordan, where a million or so refugees from Palestine have existed since 1949. Did he have work? Yes, a little, in electrical repairing, now and then he found work. A gust of wind swept by, and I must have shivered a little again. Not quickly, and not hesitatingly either, but as a natural response to this, he started to take off his coat and give it to me. I have never forgotten that move. But a little later—what else was there for me to do?—I said good-bye, and moved off. After a while he got up and went slowly on along beside the water, against the refuse-laden wind.

Farther along, near the St. George Hotel, with darkness

falling, another young man in shabby clothes came busily up to me, and speaking in loud G.I. English handed me his card:

Tourist Guide   Interpreter
Mohammad Arif
"Harry"
146932
Dependable   Modest
Fees

"You want to see Beirut at night? You like to find girl? You want to go to Turkish bath? Gay bar? You want—"

I said I was just taking a walk.

"Don't you want anything?"

Saying "no" to a question as all-encompassing as that seemed un-American, so I said, "Sure, but not tonight."

"You're in oil business?"

"No, not the oil business."

Just then two boys, one perhaps fourteen, the other harder to place—ten, perhaps, or twelve—hurried up. The younger one was very dark, with very white teeth, and something squat, monkeylike about him that suggested he might be older than he looked. He began rapidly spilling out some story to the guide, bubbling, cackling, joking, eyes flashing in dark merriment.

"This is Cheetah," the guide said, "named for the monkey in the Tarzan movie."

Cheetah extended a longish arm and shook hands, grinning impishly and making small gurgling noises.

"And this is Tarzan," the guide said, introducing the other. "They love to steal, especially the English." After a moment I realized that "from" had been left out of that sentence, but that improved it very little. The three of them plunged into gay conversation in Arabic, and the guide at one point pulled a fairly long knife out of his pocket and made playful passes across Cheetah's throat with it.

And then, as in a crude play, two sedate middle-aged Englishmen slowly strolled into view.

Tarzan and Cheetah were instantly on either side of them, Cheetah taking his Englishman's hand trustingly in his own, smiling lovingly up at him and jabbering softly. The men were so surprised that at first they didn't react but continued strolling along stiffly under close escort.

Out of the shadows and from alleys and from walls other dark young shapes stole in around this foursome, beginning to cry, "You buy chewing gum, chewing gum?" and "Welcome, welcome!" and "Beirut beautiful!" and to rattle things and scuffle and to work up a crescendo of noise and confusion around the Englishmen and as this planned chaos climbed swiftly to a rattling climax Cheetah's long arm stole toward his prey's pocket. At last seeming to awake, the Englishman shoved him smartly away and the ragged group fell back a little; Cheetah looked genuinely stricken and hurt. The two visitors hesitated for only a moment and then headed briskly back toward the St. George Hotel, accompanied by dwindling cries from the street boys.

Losing interest, the guide beside me said, "Some other night you come with me. I am here every night until six A.M."

"Six P.M.?"

"Six A.M. Six in the morning. I live on this street. It's wonderful." He turned his lifeless young face toward the sea. "Like an animal." I started on. "Go with God," he said in a habitual tone.

My Lebanese acquaintance came for me in his racing car, and we careened up to his palace.

It sat on a hillside surrounded by gardens and cypresses, a balustraded terrace running the length of the facade overlooking the Mediterranean. Inside, thin Turkish colonnades supported the very high, very richly colored ceilings, thick winy rugs warmed the marble floors, one marble wing contained a great stairwell with niches where, behind glass, bits of ancient pottery and art objects found on the property were illuminated. "You'll know much more about those than I will," my host said a little helplessly. I wondered why he should think that. Servants in white robes and turbans glided soundlessly from great room to great room. Cushions, cushions, and more mountains of cushions; incense sticks trailing tails of smoke and vapors of the East; vast family portraits and beautiful screens; space and silence and serenity. We settle into a corner of the great library, the soft lamplight throwing shadows toward the ceiling. "Will you have champagne?" he asked politely. "I only drink champagne myself." Again, it was like a line from a crude play; there was no artful restraint in Beirut, it was all melodrama. I said I would have champagne too. He was a very kind man and we talked for a while, and then he asked me to explain his country to him. "Tell me what you've seen of Lebanon up to now. Such a baffling country. Explain it to me." I told him what I had seen of Lebanon so far. "Yes, yes," he said a shade unhappily. "I don't understand it all."

This helplessness turned out to be a performance, designed maybe to put others at their ease, to spare them the discomfiture of meeting nakedly the steel-trap mind behind it. "You have, of course, been everywhere," he rambled on. "What's going on in the world? We here in our backwater. . . ."

My first impulse had been to bring up the street boys, and the people living in the hovels behind my apartment, and like a real American reformer in this sultanesque setting somehow query my host on what he and the country were doing about these wretched lives on his doorstep. He might be doing many things for all I knew. But then I remembered that there were thirty million Americans living in real, true poverty, and what was I, what were we, doing about them in the richest country in the world? So I let that subject go.

Later we got into the racing car again and went to a party of Beirut intellectuals. There was a pert middle-aged playwright who had a success running in Paris at the moment, and pretty ladies and slim young men and serious girls. They all spoke the fastest French I had ever heard. From there I was taken to another party in a sumptuous apartment that seemed to be all hushed lamps and rich rugs and glass walls. Here the people were all very good-looking, their clothes even more Parisian, and the French was even faster and no one was allowed to finish saying anything. What I could grasp from the conversation seemed to concern faithless lovers and confidence tricks, and high-society murders. From there we went to a nightclub in a cellar. The entertainment was in the middle of the dance floor and consisted of a girl in pants doing a portrait of a strong-faced Lebanese man with a thick black mustache, who was sitting for her. Surrounding them the young art set jabbered away. Photographers from a Beirut newspaper busily photographed everything. After she had achieved a creditable likeness she took a tube of electric pink paint and brutally laid this color in an X pattern across it. Then she turned the painting upside down and began to fill in sections of the design with raw purples and greens. Slowly the portrait disappeared under layers of blazing paint. From there we went to the television station where one of the group, a beautiful blonde French girl, did an announcement lasting a couple of minutes, and then we went to a huge Arab café where men sat grimly at tables watching women belly dance to whining music and from there we went to a house not quite as large as the first palace to raid the kitchen and from there we went to the red-light district near the heart of town where very ugly women huddled over little lights in huts and waited. In one hideous alley I passed the young guide who was trying to start a conversation with two Americans.

Beirut was chaos. I met a charming lady portrait painter from England and an intellectual, super-sophisticated Parisian writer and an eighteen-year-old Druze from the mountains and the tourist guide and Donna Linda Sursock in her palace where the famous accident of the ambassador falling into the fountain took place and I met a young Moslem whose foot was nearly shot away by Christians in the uprising of 1958 and a contemptuous young German who disliked every last detail of the country and a rarely emancipated Arab girl dressed with Greenwich-Village grimness whose novel *I Live!* had created a local stir and doubtless shocked the Moslems and I met a middle-aged, adventurous American couple who had the American talent for informal hospitality and friendship and two young Lebanese who looked exactly —but precisely—alike but legally had no relationship whatever and a nice old Austrian lady married to a deposed Iraqi diplomat and an American diplomat who claimed his young son had been "stoned" by jealous neighbors' children and a man who showed sex movies and an aged Near-Eastern thinker who answered every question with a paradox and a homesick young English doctor and I met Elsa Maxwell and each of them seemed to have as much, and as little, claim on Beirut as anyone else. Even the tall and brooding and handsome son of a great Lebanese fortune had grown up in New York State, and the Druze from the hills was as foreign to Beirut almost as I was, with his frontier-crossing tribal loyalties, and even the Moslem wounded in the uprising felt only a provisional connection with the city, and all the intellectuals felt that really they were only living in the most distant of all Paris suburbs, and no one could belong or wanted to belong firmly to Beirut except perhaps the young wolves of the streets, who slept on her stones at night.

All that made me feel more approving of New York City, where I had been living. Its life has been steadily criticized for years for its shifting currents, lack of neighborliness, lack of stability, and rootlessness. In Beirut I saw that at least it was not alone.

And do people really want and need roots today? Why is "rootlessness" considered such an undesirable state? We're not plants. People with "strong roots" are just as often stunted and twisted by them as not. What the human race wants is not to be rooted or rootless but flourishing, and isn't rootlessness the right way to achieve that now, for the West Virginian loafing workless in his coal town for whom there is a good factory job in Cleveland, and the engineer from Iowa who is bored by the unimportance of what he's doing there but who is desperately needed in Alaska, and wasn't the Vicks man from Florence who was afraid of Paris out of step with the times, because of his strong, and binding, Florentine roots?

Roots are supposed to be good because of their important role in the past. Nomadism has had a great deal older, and just as honored a role, and still had in certain places where I was about to go. We're inventing a new form of nomadism in the 1960's because that's what's called for, the only difference from classic nomadism being that this time we can't roam in tribes with all our sisters and our cousins and our aunts—which may be just as well—this time we—the writer and the engineer and the coal miner and the excess farmer and so on and so on—have to go out as a single family, or alone.

The soil of Lebanon, a rich-colored reddish-brown, surrounded and dramatized groves of Mediterranean pines, thick green clouds under the powerful sun of the Levant.

The Lebanese were interesting to look at. They were usually olive-skinned with dark, often hooded eyes, although quite a number were fair. Some of the women were darkly beautiful, with a quiet and continuous sensuality. The men were sometimes extremely handsome in the Rudolph Valentino style, but the true Lebanese male seemed to me to be the mountaineer, a striking and generic figure in white leggings rising to fan-seated pants, cloth headdress, long black mustache, strong-boned face, a lean, upright figure with a shotgun. He among the Lebanese did seem to be an authentic product of the land itself.

The best way I know of to explain Beirut is in this partial list of the schools there: the American Community School, the Armenian Evangelical Junior High School, the British Syrian Training College, Collège Dar Tarbia Wa Taalime, École Française des Sœurs de St. Vincent de Paul, Goethe Institut, the Italian School for Young Girls, the Armenian Orthodox School of the Forty Martyrs, Al-Yakzat Al Ilmieh, the Greek Good Deed School, the German Kindergarten, and the Swiss School for the Blind.

Beirut was like a large and elaborate international camping site, where national groups pitched their tents, cooked their own food, read their own books, spoke their own language, and, it seemed, would one day pack everything up and go home again.

Something was continually ticking in the back of my mind in Lebanon. What was it, what was it? Some surprising thought worked its way slowly toward the surface. In an odd way I seemed to be not discovering but instead recognizing the country; I had a kind of memory of it from somewhere; the Moorish invasion of Europe and the Crusader invasion of the Near East had left some kind of echo in me, and then, yes, there were the illustrations in Bible storybooks in my childhood which showed robes like these, and even these profiles, and cypresses and umbrella pines like these in the background, back behind Abraham and his son or some other biblical figure, and the stained-glass windows I had stared at in the bottomless torpor of boyhood church-going had illustrated these hills with these slim towers; I had stared a thousand times at them, behind the foreground figures of St. John baptizing Christ, and the country ladies with their long and pretty veils I saw on the roads in the Near East demurely riding along on donkeys were nothing less than successors to Mary herself with hardly an article of dress changed, and all of these people and their country and their architecture were part of my earliest childhood memories, and not quite believing what was happening at first, I gradually began to feel eerily at home in the East.

Part

DAMASCUS AMMAN
WADI RUMM
PETRA JERUSALEM

Three

In September, when the worst of the desert heat began to lift a little, I went inland from Lebanon to Jordan, which in my own context was like going from New York to upper Vermont. Jordanians, to put it plainly, were the hicks of the Near East, with all the simpler virtues that that implies: an ingenuousness which was very rare in the area, a hospitableness, and most of all, among the really basic Jordanians, an absolute enchantment with foreigners. I had the experience rather often in Jordan of being gaped at frankly as if I were some kind of natural wonder, like a talking porpoise; passing through the security check at King Hussein's palace gates one day I saw that one of the Sten-gun-carrying soldiers was eyeing me with this kind of baffled excitement, and when I happened to say a word in English he exploded with laughter. The thing talked! The notion of American omnipotence also survived there. The terrible biblical curse of the Near East, eye disease, is still a menace, and one young Jordanian asked me to help him get into a Jerusalem clinic for treatment of his bad eye. I said I would do what I could, but what could I do, as a visitor or a guest or a tourist in Jordan? "You are an American," he answered quietly.

The borders of Lebanon and Jordan don't quite meet, a corner of Israel coming between them. Frontier lines in the Near East were an even sadder exhibition of human tortuousness than even those of continental Europe, and this was heightened by the sight of the natural order and grandeur of the geography they attempted to dismember. The people felt this, and were continually on the point of falling on their borders and erasing them and forming one country or at least a federation. Smuggling seemed to rank with banking as a prestigious profession in the area, if only because it asserted this feeling of unity. Many people didn't know or care whether they were "Lebanese" or "Syrian" or "Jordanian"; they were nomads who went where the grazing was, and this applied also to highly educated people working in cities whose families had holdings in several countries.

So to get from Lebanon to Jordan I had to drive through Syria (Israel being of course closed to inter-Arab traffic), the road out of Beirut beginning to climb on the outskirts of the city and going on and up, up through the green and beautiful Lebanese mountains, down into the shining and fertile Bekaa Valley, with farmers napping in tiny straw houses on their rich fields, a promised-land land containing the great Roman provincial ruin of Baalbek, its columns the apotheosis of all columns for what that's worth, columns having a limited and decreasing meaning and beauty as the traveler ages and hardens, the road then climbing again up through the Anti-Lebanon Mountains to the flimsy frontier structures, and past those into a thin-soiled upland of rolling hills and scrub growth: Syria.

Damascus. My room in the Omayyad Hotel looked down on a respectable-residential street of modernistic light gray buildings, where students in Western-style clothes went by to school. There was also a lot of very noisy traffic in the street. The hotel quickly revealed itself to be in the bad deluxe class. That the Arabs had no talent for running hotels was becoming clear to me: they only seemed to be able to entertain people well when they meant it, when they did it personally in their homes or in their tents; they didn't seem capable of providing good impersonal service to strangers.

Two American press correspondents were with me. Both were the sole representatives in the area of very important American publications. They both were unusually vague people, and one seemed partly insane. I liked them both very much, but the borderline case, Oscar, I liked better, with his full, flushed face, the paranoic glitter of his eyes, his uncontrollable hair, and his constant squirming: he was sitting on top of an emotional volcano and knew that at any moment it might blow him sky-high. The three of us had driven together from Beirut to Damascus, and the other correspondent, Pete, murmured as a joke halfway across Lebanon, "Everybody have his passport?" Oscar, who had been a foreign correspondent for at least a decade and who had crossed so many frontiers that the extra pages in his passport made it look like a bloated accordion, shrieked, "Oh my God!" his full face falling, his high color heightening, eyes bulging, "Oh my God!" convulsively going through his pockets, "It *must* be here! I *must* have it! Look on the floor! Isn't it there under the back seat somewhere? Do you think I put it in the trunk? Oh what a dumb shit I am! Do either of *you* have it?" saying this a shade suspiciously. "Search your pockets. It's *got* to be here! I could kill myself! I *know* it's here somewhere, I *know* it is!"

Back to Beirut, back to his hotel we went, and then set out again on the road to Damascus, which we traversed uneventfully this time except for a temper fit by Oscar when one of the Syrian frontier guards attempted a routine check. "Their spy will put a tail on us as soon as we get to the hotel," he said darkly.

At the hotel Oscar and Peter excavated a congressman from Pennsylvania, and the four of us retired to the lounge for an interview on the Near East. We sat looking at each other for a while, the two correspondents clearing their throats and doodling, until to break the silence I began interviewing the congressman myself. He, however, happened not to know anything about the Near East, and to cover his silences he began to interview Oscar and Pete. They suddenly opened up and submitted happily to the interview and gave the congressman quite a few good quotes which, for all I know, he later inserted in the *Congressional Record*. Then they set out to cover Damascus.

No one they wanted to see was in, or if in not available, or if available not obliging, or if obliging not informed, and while Pete persevered Oscar returned to the hotel and interviewed me, not about the Near East but about myself. The whole thing was a joke, of course.

"Why do you write?" he demanded.

"For money."

"What's your next book about?"

"Sex."

"What are you doing here?"

"Spying for Arthur Schlesinger, Jr."

"Why for Arthur Schlesinger, Jr.?"

"Because I happened to meet him just before I left and he told me to write him if I learned anything he should know, and I've been trying to find out something Arthur Schlesinger, Jr., should know."

"Have you succeeded?"

"Yes."

"What did you find out?"

"That the American press is going to hell in the Near East."

His laugh had a certain briefness, and I caught his eye then, and some new, deeper gleam in it transmitted to me the startling information that he was taking this interview seriously and asking himself whether I had any news value at all and whether he had better cable these views to America.

"Listen!" I interrupted. "I'm kidding, you understand that, don't you?"

"Um-hum," he twiddled his pencil and gazed into the middle distance, "sure."

So there was nothing to do but go through the whole interview again, stating that I wrote to explain what I felt about life to myself, and to communicate that to other people, and to use a talent I thought I had, and, yes, also for money, that my next book was about—well, I was stuck there, as so many authors are—that it was not about sex but about mistrust and weakness and self-sacrifice and liberation (big words, but it takes big ones to bury "sex"), that I was not a spy and not working for Arthur Schlesinger, Jr., and that the American press in the Near East was a marvel of competence.

I never knew whether he believed me, but I was saved by not being news.

Then Oscar and I went to the bazaar. He needed to furnish his apartment in Cairo and had decided to buy many things here in Damascus where there did seem to be many fine household things to buy, and while he was at it he was going to teach the wiliest Arabian bargainer in the Damascus bazaar that this time he had met his match. I don't know how many stalls we contemptuously walked out of, how many times our car began to pull very very slowly away from rug merchants' doors, how many lightninglike revisits we made to glance at tables Oscar would just tolerate buying, disappointing as he loudly claimed they were, if his price was met. His combined-attack technique of outrageously low offers, one tenth of the asking price, for instance, uninterruptible criticism of the goods' quality, sudden departures, doubled or tripled the time consumed in buying and, it seemed to me, saved him nothing except tiny discounts pityingly conceded to save his face by these masters of the bazaar. Oscar.

As we dashed along the tricky turnings, through the crowded arcades full of cries and spicy smells, the robes and veils and shadows of Damascus, Oscar, scooting along in the style created by Groucho Marx, poured out to me intense tales of his sex life in the Far East. "Delicate, doll-like creatures, jade or ivory, hands like little birds, little tiny ivory birds, but what *things* these teeny delicate birds can do, and they sit there opposite you like little goddesses, all fragile and graceful and all that, and you remember how ancient their civilization is and that we were clobbering each other with clubs when they were contemplating high Confucian philosophical thought, and you feel all humble and inferior and adoring because nothing makes me adore something more than feeling inferior to it—that's one of my complexes—and just when I'm almost hypnotized by her grace and civilization and all that this big greasy piece of gristle comes twisting out of her mouth like some kind of a snake—ugh—the end. Take it from me, don't ever eat with them, it'll shatter every illusion. Gristle! Ugh."

Like all people with his mania, Oscar assumed that every experience of his life was directly and immediately useful to others. It was no use saying that I doubted I would ever go to the Far East, *Oscar had been there,* and the wisdom he brought back was of instant, universal value, "The climate'll kill you, but if you get clothes in this store in Hong Kong I'll tell you about—"

"Oscar," I would try to say calmly and quietly and reasonably, "I'm never going to go to the Far East."

"—you won't be sweating all night *and* day out there. Good material. Look. These pants, they come from there, and I got them for $3.17. Wash them myself, and hang them out on the bamboo shoots to dry. Ten minutes. Here we are! No, for Christ's sake don't stop; no don't look, come on, right on by, *here's* where we stop, his competitor's. Yes, that's a nice piece of jewelry, I could send that to Waving Grain or whatever her name was, the gristle girl, ugh, she likes this kind of worked silver, *now* we go, slowly, slowly, we just *inch* our way back to that stall where he's got the *really* good stuff."

This kept on until well after dark, and I remember standing in the Street Called Straight—very ancient, shop-lined, narrow, long and straight, like the last corridor of civilization pointing straight on to the huge heartland of Asia—Oscar and I in the dark before a little frontless room filled with beautiful rugs, the merchant in robes beside Oscar, dignified and tricky and unbudging, and his teen-aged helper in bare feet almost as articulate as his hands, eyes like dark lamps expressionlessly watching the bargaining as he swiftly sewed with a long curving needle two panels of rug together, our car idling behind us, the bright tunnels made by the headlights leaping along the Street Called Straight. I felt that I had entered another world totally now and that it was no longer a question of liking it or not liking it, because it had me completely surrounded and had become existence itself.

The next day Oscar, the last of the expatriates, like a left-over alone and nervous at the Café du Dôme, sitting there since 1929 because no one had told him about the market crash and he never knew that the jet plane had destroyed his species, the next day Oscar left. Oscar to me was still waiting for Caresse Crosby and Harry to come back and give another marvelous party, or else the Murphys, waiting for the Black Sun Press, or Miss Stein, ready to go a round with Ernest or to her dancing lesson with Zelda, because although his playground had been the Far East he was spiritually an escapee from America in the 1920's tradition, the next day Oscar hurriedly left trailing his purchases to set up that apartment in Cairo, which would not be permanent.

There was a kind of powdery blueness and light grayness to the air in Damascus. Some of the streets were lined with small feathery trees. There was the Omayyad Mosque built twelve centuries ago in the heart of the bazaar with unforgettable vastness. These and other things added weight and size and past to my impression of this total world. Crossing the enormous court of the mosque, having taken off my shoes and been given slippers, I looked up at the minaret, which resembled in solidity a side of the Empire State Building, up to the huge balcony where tiny lost human specks cried in flamenco-like, rawly beautiful song, the call to prayer. The interior stretched away from me like a country estate, every inch of it richly rugged, chandeliers sailing in the enormous spaces above, an imam reciting from the Koran in an angry voice to a circle of seated men, one very large tomb behind a piked fence interrupting the otherwise featureless field of rugs, with a few Moslems contemplating it with religious respect: it contained the head of John the Baptist, a very revered prophet in the Moslem religion. I couldn't help remembering, amid the simplicity and mightiness of the Omayyad Mosque, the stuffy, *grand bourgeois* clutter which Westminster Abbey has become.

Then I started by car across the desert to Jordan, gripped by the remoteness I was penetrating, and then suddenly thinking what an entirely relative term "remote" was. Jordan not only was not remote to the Jordanians, but it never had been remote from, but always very close to or at, the core of their and our world, and I and my country have always been remote. Feeling slightly less important than before that platitude occurred to me, I drove on toward Amman.

Because of my mountain of books, I was no longer completely ignorant about where I was going and what had happened there and why. World history is the only kind worth teaching today: why had time been used up hearing about the Gadsden Purchase, why had I been told about Major André, although memory in its realistic way refused to retain any information on him, while I had never heard of Harun al-Rashid? Why could I to this day draw the boundaries of the Republic of Texas and, until I set foot in it, not really know where Damascus was? Was "Fifty-four forty, or fight!" a more important historical cry to fix in my mind than "There is no god but God and Mohammed is his Prophet"? The problem of the boundaries of Texas and Washington State were settled and died as a problem a long time ago, while the history and tenets of Islam are some of the most alive and influential facts in the world: they may start a world war, or turn back communism, or even overrun us still. Islam has more adherents than any religion in the world except Christianity, and America is one of the few parts of the world where they do not live in large numbers. They of course are most numerous and most powerful here at the crossroads of world geography with its strategic preeminence and here they sit on the most critical substance in the world —oil—and the United States, I found, is deeply involved in the economy and defense and future of the region and the American people know hardly anything about it.

Crossing the desert to Jordan, I now knew something about the Arab world. I knew that the Arabs entered world history in A.D. 570, when Mohammed was born in Mecca, a town in the center of the Arabian peninsula. He was a great-grandson of Hashim (which means Bread-Breaker), who established a family dynasty, the Hashemites, and became Caliph of

Mecca. The present King Hussein of Jordan is a Hashemite and a direct descendant of Hashim and of Mohammed. Arab history is not very long nor very remote from today, especially since the living habits of large numbers of Arabs have changed very little between then and now.

Mohammed grew up as an orphan, and married a wealthy widow when he was twenty-four. By her he had Fatima, his only child to have descendants. He became a moderately successful merchant of Mecca, which was, as it is today, the focal shrine of Arab religion. The religion at that time was pagan, and in Mecca worship centered on a stone building called the Kaaba, and a large meteor set in it called the Black Stone, which is still there although no longer worshiped. Mohammed's relatives were the official guardians of the holy place, and remained so until King Hussein of Jordan's great-uncle Ali was driven out by Ibn Saud in 1925.

It was a profitable position to occupy, and the family was deeply disturbed when at the age of forty Cousin Mohammed began spending a lot of time by himself in caves, where he became subject to visions. A visionary was the last thing the Meccans wanted around them: they were busily building fortunes on the caravan routes, north, east, south and west, which converged on Mecca, and making money also from the pilgrimages to their Kaaba, stuffed with every kind of idol including representations of Jesus and Mary, the catch-all shrine of a catch-all religion in which few intelligent Meccans believed any more but from which all made money. They had been a nomadic people, and this experiment in settling down and forming a town was turning out successfully. The Meccan merchants, with their camels and multiple wives, their robes and shrewdness, thought life was good enough as it was.

But Mohammed began having his visions. There always seems to be a visionary to disturb the peace just when everybody is finding life so satisfactory, always an awkward misfit crying out against the music everybody else is dancing to, always a bedraggled interloper at the banquet. Mohammed was one of that ungainly, deeply resented, usually martyred school, and without going into the question of whether he was divinely inspired or not, modern objective scholarship considers him a true visionary and mystic of deep spiritual power.

Meanwhile he was thrashing around in his cave, being visited by a Glorious Being, who was God or an Angel, perhaps Gabriel, bearing revelations which Mohammed found more and more disturbing. He, Mohammed, was to be the messenger of God, the last of the prophets, following in the divinely inspired footsteps of Abraham and Moses and John the Baptist and Christ, the culmination of God's revelations begun in Judaism and Christianity. What's more, he was to begin his mission in Mecca, with teachings which flew in the face of the life of all his friends and relatives.

And here was why disturbers of the peace such as Mohammed arise amid apparent plenty and contentment. Meccan society, beneath its busy surface prosperity, was in deep confusion about how to behave and what was good and whether it mattered. As nomads in the desert they had lived by a strong concept of personal honor, but now in the town, in commerce, the maintenance of that kind of desert honor wasn't necessary any more. A man's importance could be judged by his fortune now: be stingy, be selfish, forget family and tribal responsibilities, seize pleasure and power now because death was the end of everything.

Trembling in his cave, Mohammed was told by his visions to defy and redirect all of that. He went to his wife, the older, sympathetic Khadija; she sustained him and believed in him, and Mohammed overcame his doubts about himself and his visions, and came out to face the daunting array of forces against him, an uneducated, moderately successful middle-aged businessman, stepping forth to defy all the gods and powers of Arabia.

There is a day of atonement, he preached, when your good and bad deeds will confront you; you are going to rise from the dead some day and so now, here, you must be generous, you must worship not money but God, who is not in that crowd of idols in the Kaaba, there is only one true God, the God of Judaism and Christianity, and I am his Prophet.

What has gotten into Mohammed, the Meccans murmured to each other, Mohammed who sometimes had fits and who may or may not have been able to read and write, Mohammed who after all married money and only that way attained what success he had? Cousin Mohammed, the Prophet of God?

Everyone knows what happens to prophets in their own countries.

But Medina, two hundred and fifty miles up the caravan route, listened. Medina had been established on a fertile oasis and it suffered from spiritual confusion similar to Mecca's, with the sharper practical spur that blood feuds between families there were making life almost impossible. They heard of Mohammed and went to Mecca and talked to him, and were deeply moved. Here was a man of great spiritual authority and *not* a prophet of their own particular place, objective therefore, nonaligned, one who could judge and settle antagonisms among them fairly. They urged him to come to Medina.

At the same time, in Mecca, the second classic fate for a prophet crept toward Mohammed. His family was persuaded to withdraw its protection from him. There was no police force in the city; a citizen was protected by his family, who would retaliate against any insult made to him, and kill a member of any family that killed him. And now Mohammed was unprotected by this tradition. He had turned out to be too disturbing for everybody except a few followers; he looked like a possible political threat if his popularity grew; he was attacking the gods; the revenues seemed threatened.

He was dangerous—much more so, surely, than the ruffled merchants of Mecca could possibly have realized. If they had had an inkling of the next ten years, Mohammed would have been pulled to pieces in the streets; but then, if they had had an inkling of the next thirty, and the next hundred, they would have fallen at his feet.

Since he did not look mortally dangerous, death crept toward him but did not lunge, and with fine-spun Arab subtlety, Mohammed silently stole away, fading into the desert with a follower and two servants, on camels, deviously, in September of 622, stealing north to Medina, to his strong ranks of new believers there, to safety and incredible success, accomplishing his Hegira, from which the Moslems date time.

During the next ten years every success that Mohammed had seemed to make his character firmer, and he had little except successes. His new religion, Islam, quickly and naturally became militant under his leadership. First, all of Medina was converted, except for the Jewish sector, which Mohammed urgently wanted because he felt himself the continuer of their faith. After a complicated doctrinal struggle the Jews definitely rejected his teaching, and the schism of faith in the Near East so aflame there today began. He started leading raiding parties against the caravans of Mecca, a normal practice and almost a sport in Arabia; this culminated in a major pitched battle with the Meccans, won by Mohammed. And the size and militancy of these raids increased like a whirlwind in the desert, tribe after tribe becoming converted to Islam and therefore immune from attack, the whole concept changing from mere secular raiding into a Holy War against unbelievers which, as the whole of the Arabian peninsula began to come under Mohammed's sway, was inevitably turning outward; the Prophet's instinct for unifying the tribes of Arabia as part of their salvation had liberated them from their self-confinement; instead of dispersing all their energies on squabbles among themselves they began to turn, as one at last, outward, and at the center of this vortex of exploding energy can be seen Mohammed, revealing qualities as a diplomat, military leader, arbiter, administrator, and politician, that alone made the transformation he was achieving possible. He seems to have been self-controlled in a race of passionate men, generous amid stinginess, practical and firm and tactful in a land where these qualities were as rare as water.

The personalities of most great religious leaders disappear under layers of adulation, generation by generation, until at last little or nothing human shines through any more. This is not the case with Mohammed; in his triumphant last year of life, 632, with the miracle of a united Moslem Arabia around him, Mohammed received a communication from a Christian teacher of central Arabia. "From Musaylimah the messenger of God to Mohammed the messenger of God," it began. "From Mohammed the messenger of God," the reply opened, "to Musaylimah the liar." Around him, in Medina, were Mohammed's many wives, whom he took after his beloved first wife's death and as the necessity for alliances by marriage mounted. Rather suddenly, in 632, when he was sixty-two, Mohammed fell ill, excused himself from spending the night in succession with each of his wives, and shortly died, and was buried in Medina with a space next to his body reserved for Christ's.

Islam, which means submission to and peace with God, spread like fire, one reason for this being its simplicity. It had never claimed that Mohammed was anything more than a man, a man inspired by God. It presented only five fundamental rules of life: once in his life a Moslem (which means,

One Who Submits) must say with full understanding and acceptance, "There is no god but God, and Mohammed is his Prophet"; five times a day he must pray—at dawn, at noon, in midafternoon, at dusk, and after dark—kneeling and continually prostrating himself toward Mecca and touching his forehead to the ground to symbolize his adoration of God and submission to God; he must give alms generously, often in prescribed amounts; he must observe the month of Ramadan, when nothing may be eaten or drunk between sunrise and sunset; and finally, once in his life, if possible, he must make the pilgrimage to Mecca. The large majority of Moslems belong to the Sunnite sect, which on the whole has a tolerant philosophy. A much smaller dissident sect, the Shi'ites, are responsible for much of Islam's reputation for fanaticism. Through most of the Arab Empire, most of the time, Jews, Christians and other "nonbelievers" were left in peace by the Moslems. They were "People of the Book," mentioned by Mohammed in the Koran.

One tenet of the Islamic faith which shook the world, and may again, was that in choosing the Arabs as the people of his last prophet, God clearly was assigning to them the spiritual, and also the temporal, supremacy of the world. Out of the Arabian peninsula they poured as a result of this article of faith, and the conquests and achievements of the Arabs had begun.

Within a century they had poured east to central India and west across all of North Africa, taken Spain, and were only turned back 145 miles south of Paris, at Tours. For a long time in their conquests the Arabs of Arabia were strictly soldiers and commanders, leaving with some condescension all other functions to conquered peoples. The center of this scimitar of an empire was moved from the forbidding deserts of Arabia to Damascus under the Omayyad dynasty, and in the eighth century to Baghdad under the Abbasid dynasty.

Moslem economic influence extended from Japan to Sweden, and Islam rose above Europe and the rest of the world in prosperity and in cultural achievement. Assimilating the decaying knowledge found in their empire from Greek, Persian, Indian and other sources, the Moslems now became the leaders of civilization, establishing centers of learning in Baghdad, Cairo, Bukhara, Damascus, Aleppo, Córdoba and elsewhere, systematizing the available knowledge of the past and advancing in medicine, chemistry, astronomy, mathematics, philosophy and other fields. Córdoba had seventy libraries, three hundred public baths, miles of paved and lighted streets, when London and Paris were wallowing in mud and ignorance.

The accomplishments of Islam are always compared by Western writers to those of Europe, because the Moslems are, as Glubb Pasha had pointed out, "the closest people in the world to us," and that is the reason why "Islam" suggests "fanaticism" to the Western mind, and "Saracen" suggests "barbarian." In fact, they were never barbarians and not often fanatics. What they were was our closest and toughest rivals in the world, and that is why they have been seen as ogres by the West. No one has ever pretended that they were paragons of gentleness. But no one who looks at their history and exploits, or lives among them today, can think of them as ogres. To an aggressive younger boy, however, the bigger fighter next door always looks like an ogre.

No sooner had the Arab Empire reached its fabulous limits than it began to fragment, because of the immemorial Arab trait, visible today, of inability to combine with one another and agree on sustained united action.

And so barbarians from the east and west began to prey on the decomposing empire, beginning with the first Crusades invasion in 1096, and then—much more dangerous—with the Mongols from the east, who were only stopped, when they had penetrated to Palestine, by the militant Turkish garrison of Egypt called the Mamelukes. Meanwhile, through the Crusades and through Arab realms in Sicily and Spain, the cultural treasures assembled by Islam began to filter through to benighted Europe and to prepare the way for its Renaissance and achievement of civilization.

At the same time, disunity and confusion and political instability were hacking at the foundations of the great Arab Empire; the ingenious irrigation engineering which brought out the riches of the Tigris and Euphrates valleys fell into a neglect and ruin that is only being repaired today; lordly Damascus was being beaten down by revolts and misgovernment and corruption, its schools and hospitals and cultural centers sliding toward extinction; scholarly Alexandria lost track of its thoughts; Black Death and famine drastically cut into the already reeling population; and from the Turkish peninsula, where the Arabs had recruited so many garrisons for their Empire, where the people were disciplined while the Arabs were individualistic, unimaginative while the Arabs liked to speculate, tyrannical while the Arabs were aristocratic, from their peninsula the Turks spread an imperial dominance over a now exhausted Arab-Moslem world, and the great Arab adventure went to sleep.

It was awakened with a start as the nineteenth century opened, by jabs from Europe, beginning with Napoleon's invasion of Egypt in 1798, and, later on, more lasting British incursions. Their shock on awakening has been called "cosmic," and the Moslem world has not recovered from it yet. Had not the Prophet himself, the apex of all truth, said to them: "You are the best community that has been brought forth for mankind"? And still here were these unbelieving Europeans parading proudly into their land, far ahead of them in a great many undeniable ways. Had Mohammed been wrong? It was as shocking a question to face as a devout

Christian asking himself, "Was Christ wrong?" And that is why Westerners find Moslems "touchy"; Moslems are balanced painfully between genuine admiration for Western achievement and a troubling need to reject that achievement, a devastating need both from religious belief and natural egotism to prove themselves supreme once again, to be what they once undeniably were, the best community.

I realized that much about the Moslem state of mind, so I said to myself on entering their world: I'm not going to criticize anything. And I didn't for nearly two months. The worst food, the most fly-bitten alley, the thickest dust storm: through everything I went without a murmur. I began to feel rather proud of myself. Perhaps subconsciously I began saying to myself: Whatever the best community in the world is, I belong to it. Finally, at dinner one night, in a kind of airplane-hangar dining room in Amman, with a floor show of a girl in tights firing blanks at her acrobatic partner in a bearskin, parts of which lit up now and then, dining with a purple-faced European, one of the emotionally unstable free-lance businessmen who infest the Near East, like the dregs of the last Crusade, and a gentle and intelligent young Jordanian, in order to keep the European from completely smothering the conversation, and in order to feel a little less perfect, I let myself criticize the look of the Church of the Holy Sepulcher in Jerusalem. After all, I reasoned to myself, it has only been in Jordanian territory since 1949, it is ours, a Christian church built and maintained by Christians. So I criticized something in the Near East. The Jordanian, who had been daily offering me every hospitality, never saw me again.

Everything is close together in the Near East, much closer than I had dreamed. The trip by car from the capital of Lebanon, Beirut, to the capital of Syria, Damascus, took just two hours. From Damascus to the capital of Jordan, Amman, by car took four hours. You could drive the length of Jordan in six hours, and the length of the advance of Lawrence of Arabia from his first victory at Aqaba to his last at Damascus, which took him two years, in eight hours. This made everywhere seem accessible, as if you could hold a country in the palm of your hand and encompass it physically, as is inconceivable in the United States; the sense an American has of wallowing blindly in our huge spaces didn't exist here; there is the capital, and over there is the other principal city, and that line of hills is the frontier, and over there is the seacoast. "Cozy" was not the word for these countries at all, "stark" was much closer, but there was this sense of closeness about them which must be another reason why they were constantly toying with the idea of union; they are on top of each other already.

In Jordan I was immediately engulfed in conversations on politics, in Amman, and on religion, in Jerusalem. Nothing else was going on. Both topics quickly wore thin because they revolved endlessly around disputes which appeared absolutely insoluble, and so I turned from them as much as possible to look at the country and at the people on their nonpolitical and nonreligious sides.

My first night in the country I went to sleep in the Hotel Philadelphia in Amman. It is famous, in the way that Radio City Music Hall is famous, as an experience not to be missed during a visit although not necessarily enjoyed. I fell asleep in my small room which looked out on the palm trees in front of the hotel, and beyond them on a steep, partially restored Roman amphitheater across the street. I slept for a long time and then I heard a flat but musical man's voice singing, the lone clear sound sailing down through the steep sleeping canyons of Amman in the moonlight, and sitting up in bed in wonderment I peered out the window at the classical theater slumbering under the moon, white, silent, empty, ageless, and in bewilderment—where am I? I can't remember what country this is after all this travel—I looked across the moonlighted room and thought: That's a great canopy there, and there is a Hashemite prince asleep in there, I don't know which one—Hussein or Feisal or Abdullah—and this is a tent, and we are in the desert. Those are other tents down there under the palms, and it seems to be a peaceful night out here in the desert with nobody to bother us, the guard wouldn't be singing if there was any danger, and the prince, the Hashemite prince there, is peacefully asleep.

The hallucination continued for a while and then faded, and I went back to sleep and the next morning pieced together that the muezzin and the moonlight and the amphitheater had been real, and that the canopy bed had been a wardrobe and that the tents had been cars.

That night I went to the old theater with Colonel Ramayah. The name of the theater, mysteriously, was Pharaoh's Daughter's Stairs.

Colonel Ramayah was the first Jordanian I got to know. "Misser Nolss?" he said, coming up to me on the Hotel Philadelphia's intrigue-ridden front porch, his desert warrior's head hanging shyly, "You like to see Addab dances?" I said I would, and so across the street to the Roman amphitheater we walked through an atmosphere combining a movie premiere with a major political assassination. Crowds, revolving lights in the darkness, barricades, drums meshed and clashed in the night as the Colonel and I went to seats in the first circle near the great central raised stone stage. That was the opening clue to what Colonel Ramayah was like: he always got the best seats in the house.

Except for the King's, of course. Hussein sat behind a rug-draped balustrade in the center of the semicircle, another rug underfoot, with a small table at his knees where a servant served small cups of coffee; his new wife beside him—an English girl, twenty years old—and behind and around them, high up into the very steep ancient theater, a dark and uncontainable throng of Jordanians was swept by those unknowable tides of emotion Arabs experience in theaters. On the stage, all but effaced by the dark glamour of the audience, Lebanese folk dancers did their best, the men in black boots, black Arab pants, white and black striped shirts and turban-like hats, moving slowly together with their arms over one another's shoulders, forward, down, up, sideways, back, slowly, BANG, the bootheels crashed down in unison, the orchestra music below them throbbing and whining, the girls coming on in silken trousers, blouses and transparent coats, white veiled headdresses, moving sideways, spin, forward, forward, and in unison with the men BANG, then breaking into lines of ten or so with a man leading at one end, leaping and turning in added variations, whirling in his free hand a handkerchief at shoulder level, the excitement steadily mounting, twirl, down, sideways, twirl, BANG, forward toward the audience they came, mounting mounting, a swoop, whirl, sideways, up, up, BANG ending with the control of a well-trained horse suddenly pulling up from a gallop and standing motionless in a little rising dust.

The audience meanwhile was roaring and chanting and some voice high in the seats seemed to be reciting chants in praise of King Hussein, and then a kind of comedian in traditional Turkish clothes took the stage and apparently also praised the King *in extenso* and in depth.

The ancient theater reverberated with laughter and applause; it had not heard much of either since the days when Amman had been one of the great frontier League of Ten Cities of the Roman Empire, and called Philadelphia, then was swept into the Arab Empire in the seventh century, and then into decay and emptiness beginning in the thirteenth, sleeping on forgotten and forgetful until King Hussein's grandfather Abdullah came to town in 1919 bringing the modern world with him. So here we were this night, the grandson at the center of the arc of the ancient amphitheater, where Roman governors must have sat, and then Arab sheikhs, and there before us were sword dancers stamping and clashing, and I suddenly realized, with a flashing sense of unreality, that I had deeply penetrated an alien, not to say hostile culture, that except for the King's wife there might be no other non-Arab here, and was I, I suddenly asked myself, entirely safe here or not? I continued to stare fixedly at the sword dancers; these were the dances and this was the music and this was the uproar and excitement across the lines among the Moslems; sounds and notes and cries like these might have drifted across Palestine to some Crusader ancestor of mine, and scared him by their seeming barbarity; before me and on all sides of me were the "fanatical infidels" we even today vaguely remember and vaguely, vestigially still fear in a way.

"Iss a dance of the warrior, you see," said Colonel Ramayah with a small, depreciating smile on his tough face. "You like it?" he asked hesitatingly, "Misser Nolss?"

And with the direct question asked, I suddenly knew the answer. "Yes," I said slowly, formulating my feelings as I went along, "I do. They look happy dancing up there, don't they. And the expressions on their faces. They're young people having a good time, that's what they are, isn't it." That's what they are and were and always had been, and I was experiencing the exhilarating sensation of fear—a fear I hadn't really been aware of—evaporating, the fear of the unknown, of the bogeyman, of the dark, of the otherness of strange people.

"Probably tomorrow," the Colonel said, expansively now, with a big grin, "I will show you some of Jordan, some of the nice things in Jordan, probably tomorrow."

I had met Colonel Ramayah through some American friends who lived in Beirut, and I slowly discerned his story, like tracks in the sand, overlain, windblown, but still faintly traceable in certain long slanting rays of the sun, discerned his story by working backwards from what he now was, a successful businessman with two cars and a chauffeur and a large stone house, an eighteen-year-old son and presumably a wife or two or three somewhere behind the curtains, a curved, broken-looking nose and black mustache, black hair, eyes close to the surface with eyebrows which tended to form an apex, a smiling, bearish, soft-spoken, bull-bodied man, who might, I felt, be capable of anything. I did not know whether to trust him more, or less, than anyone else in Jordan. People began to mention his "trouble" to me after a few weeks, then something about his having been under house arrest for two years. In the same breath as they mentioned he had been King Hussein's aide and at the same time, it appeared that he was in and out of the palace constantly now. And then the trouble about his legs: wasn't it fine that the paralysis caused by the torment suffered by such a man enclosed within his own four walls for two years, that that paralysis had been cured at the King's expense? And stifling an urge to grab my informant, if that is the word, by the shirtfront and shout, "*Why* was he arrested for two years? How can he have been so close to the King, and still be, and yet be punished by Jordan to the point of being crippled?" sensing that a direct question would shoot down this carrier pigeon of garbled information, I nodded slowly, and I realized then why Lawrence Durrell had had to write four novels, each contradicting and correcting the one before, in an effort to explain and express life in Alexandria. I felt that there was not going to be any Answer to questions in the Near East, and that even to ask them was to put yourself off the path toward the truth, to risk walking head-on into a tree, and that in the Near East you could only follow as the trail revealed itself before you, that it was a labyrinth and that it did not have any end anywhere. Had Colonel Ramayah, bosom friend of the King's as he was, turned against the King as Hussein's even closer friend, Ali Abu Nuwar, chief of staff of the Jordan Army, had during the Army revolt of 1957, but been spared from death by Hussein out of past friendship, and now been completely forgiven? Or had he been unflinchingly loyal always, and only imprisoned in his house by Hussein in order to protect him from the true traitors, who would have trapped and killed him in the open? Or had Hussein, convinced of the Colonel's treachery, imprisoned instead of shot him out of lingering affection—just as he had exiled instead of executed Ali Abu Nuwar—and then later gotten proof of the Colonel's innocence and so freed him and provided the cure for the terrible result of the undeserved imprisonment, paralysis of the legs? All three of these conjectures were partially indicated by what people told me or let drop in front of me or suggested by a changing expression on their faces.

And now another Near Eastern mystery seemed less mysterious: Oscar and Pete. Surely they had been assigned here because really sane, competent journalists would disintegrate trying to cover this part of the world, where there did not seem to be any final truth, not only that, there did not seem to be any firm facts. Only dreamers like Oscar and Pete could retain what sanity they had here. I imagined the first sentence of a newspaper story about Colonel Ramayah's liberation, answering the required questions of American journalism: who, what, when, where, why.

"Colonel Ahmed Ramayah, once-trusted intimate of King Hussein of Jordan, now reportedly restored to favor, which according to some observers he never lost, was rumored lately freed from a two-year house arrest ordered by the King as punishment for disloyalty, or else to protect him." Only

Oscar, eyes bulging, face flushed, hair snapping with electricity, could type that lead and still feel satisfied with himself.

Colonel Ramayah came across the front porch the next day, a gentle bear, smiling shyly. "You like to go to Jerusalem?" he asked.

I wasn't quite ready for that question: it was in the same category as seeing "Mr. Forster" painted on the door in King's College. It was, in other words, outrageous. I knew that Jerusalem was a two-hour ride from here, just as I had known that Mr. Forster lived in King's College, but when these facts entered prosaic everyday life they were too much for it, like boulders dropped in a puddle. Soon someone will have to say to our children, "Do you want to go to the moon?" to get the same reaction.

"Yes," I answered slowly, "I'd like to go to . . . Jerusalem."

Colonel Ramayah had one unusually small and one very large car. We took the latter; he dispensed with the chauffeur and drove it himself. The car was an Edsel, and finding it—and in fact many other Edsels—in Amman seemed just right, exactly the place for them. I don't mean by that that the Ford Motor Company, after the Edsel failed and was discontinued, decided to ship them off and dump them in the most out-of-the-way place it could think of—Jordan—although perhaps it did. But it was the Edsel's appropriateness as an ambitious failure that struck me, a car fashioned very well for a period that had just ended, named for an exceptional man whom destiny cast in the wrong role; all of that seemed symbolic of Jordan, and of King Hussein.

The All-Purpose Spy watched us as we pulled out of the Hotel Philadelphia's driveway. He operated a small shop in Amman as a front for his profoundly unreliable espionage intrigues. No one ever had a more unfortunate face for his profession: he looked ridiculously tricky, his long bloodhound's eyes were bottomlessly shifty as he told you what time it was, his voice dripped with a kind of whining, lying, falsetto evil, his long, lined, mud-colored face constantly smirked, a smirk which suggested both that he didn't believe a word anybody said to him and also that people who believed a word he sold them were fools. He was deeply irritating to talk to or even say "hello" to, because he managed to convey always the view that whatever you said, such as "hello," was a lie and he knew what you *really* meant.

He sold information on Jordan to Israel, and information on Israel to Jordan, Egypt, Syria and Saudi Arabia. He worked for both the Soviet Union and the United States. He was also employed by Egypt against Jordan, and by Jordan against Egypt. He came and went in the employ of Saudi Arabia depending on which Arab country their government happened to consider the current enemy. The British hired him during a crisis to buy information about everybody else. He was in fact one huge, lying clearinghouse; and more than that he too was a symbol: I came to think of him as Information itself in the Near East, as the grubby heap from which all of us interested in facts fumbled to drag one out.

His hound's face slid into an even more sardonic look than habitual as he watched Colonel Ramayah and me leaving the Philadelphia; he was sure there was a plot, probably revolutionary, behind this car ride, and he wanted us to know that he knew all about it.

The black Edsel was spacious and solid; I believe it was one of the last manufactured; the bad first frills had been eliminated and it was an excellent, powerful car. We passed Pharaoh's Daughter's Stairs, past the bust stop where Jordanian men sat on the dusty sidewalk in their long white dresses, business-suit jackets, and headcloths, waiting for the rattling bus. At the corner we crossed the "river," a trickle of water wandering through town, and turned into the main street, passing on our left public scribes writing letters at tables on the sidewalk. The main street was lined with low stone stores selling the clothes and food and hardware found anywhere, camera shops and a little jewelry bazaar, the prevailing color of the street a chalk white and light gray; we drove along it to the central square with a monument in the center and the principal mosque, then up a street on the right past modern stone buildings and out into the hills around Amman, improbable lifeless hills which looked like plaster scraped by a huge wire brush.

And there sat Colonel Ramayah, his strong head full of the intrigues and tortures and redemption he had passed through, the only person who really could explain this terrible and representative Near-East tale to me, and I wanted very much to hear it. It never occurred to me then that I would ever write about it, I merely wanted to know as part of a bottomless curiosity I had about people's lives, which combined with a dust-closet memory, a memory for example of where an acquaintance of mine spent a two-week vacation twenty years ago. My mother has a ladderlike memory on which every important date in the life of her family, her very large circle of friends and a huge outer circle of acquaintances is exactly placed, but my memory stores not When, but What. What had truly happened to Colonel Ramayah?

"Uh—Colonel Ramayah?"

"Misser Nolss?"

"Colonel, you . . . how did you like living in England?"

"England was very, very nice. I like in England."

"And did the King like England too?"

He seemed to increase the already formidable speed of the Edsel. "His Majesty King Hussein was very, very happy in England."

"You were his aide at that time, and did you continue to be for long after you came back to Jordan? Sir?"

"I'm sorry?" A glance at me from the formidable planes of his face, his foot sank harder on the accelerator and the Edsel tore across Jordan toward the Dead Sea, holding the road splendidly.

I meditated on the Colonel for a few breath-taking miles and then said in passing, "King Hussein certainly seems to be a happily married man."

After a pause he said, "His Majesty King Hussein is happy, I am told."

"She's a very pretty girl."

"Her Gracious Ladyship Muna el Hussein is very beautiful."

"He must be one of the bravest men in the world. When you remember that he walked into the middle of that army mutiny with bullets whistling past him—"

Colonel Ramayah shot out his right arm and pulled something from the open glove compartment and shoved it under the dashboard, and in a moment very loud, whining Arab music flooded the car. It was from an automoble record player, and that ended the interview.

Later I regretted repaying Colonel Ramayah's hospitality by prying into something in his life which it could only be painful or dangerous to talk about. His manners were too good for him openly to silence me.

And my American manners? Not very good, I concluded, after noticing myself in a Near-Eastern context. I didn't go through all the considerate motions others went through, and neither did the few other Americans there. We didn't write the considerate thank-you note, or give the thoughtful present, or notice that the light was shining disagreeably in someone's eyes, or defer to someone else's feelings always, or greet an acquaintance fully, undistractedly, when meeting him at a crowded gathering; we didn't focus our goodwill in the way people around us did.

Why was this? I knew the answer in my own case, at least. I grew up being afraid of insincerity as of a disease; I grew up with a revulsion against seeing a jagged smile and hearing a flat note in a compliment, a revulsion as though these insincerities were threats to life itself, which as a matter of fact I felt they were and still feel they are. Few things are more confusing as you grow up than discovering yourself surrounded by an apparent affection which you cannot however trust, unstable treacherous affection, and the result of this for me was that I refused to forge affection.

So my manners tended to be variable and American. They were an expression of a concept of honesty, a concept which the Old World finds crude, banal, irritating, and immature. The thing I had feared growing up was "phoniness," and I think this is true for many Americans and accounts for a brusqueness in our manners.

Colonel Ramayah, inexhaustibly patient and quietly polite, had grown up in a different tradition. When two Arab men of more or less equal status meet, the exchange of formula compliments and polite, set inquiries can go on for minutes on end, all the while a considerate, receptive smile lighting their faces. It is a graceful, patriarchal performance, two such men, bearded perhaps, holding their robes around them, the Arab headdress framing their faces, as they deferentially converse. The long, smiling exchange of compliments may be staged, but it is not "phony." The two men are being disarming literally: they are disarming each other. Feuds in Jordan are to the death. In the last analysis, your life there can depend on your good manners. In America we don't kill people who cut us; neither do they of course in Jordan, but it is still true that an insult there, if it is bad enough, can be mortal.

From living in Jordan I saw how economical our life in America was, the curlicues of politeness and the ceremonies of society sliced away because we hadn't time for them any more and were embarrassed by them anyway; the interminable, rambling family dinners which the youth of the Old World endure with such suffering have been done away with among us. For the first time I glimpsed why young people of other countries were attracted by America. Until then, I couldn't see why any foreigner would want to visit us; we had no old castles, comparatively little history, hardly anything picturesque; we had nothing but, well, ordinary places where people lived in the present. Who could be interested in that?

The youth of the world, I began to see the more I traveled, was fascinated by exactly that. They saw in us what the potentialities of our present—which was their future—were, and they were thrilled by them, if only because that *was* the future, almost without regard to whether it was good or bad, an advance or a retreat ethically or culturally or in any other way; they wanted it because it was going to be, that was all.

There was an impatience among the young people I met in Europe and the Near East, as though they all felt instinctively that there wasn't *time* any more for the endless family dinner and the ritual family outing on Sunday, that there was far too much now to be learned and done in the world for the lugubrious visit to grandmother and the ceremonial calls on short-tempered aunts. The young people I am thinking of were all well-educated and polite and they disliked being in conflict with their families, so they went through the required rituals but looking oddly awkward as they did it, as though they were masquerading in some costume out of past history. They urgently wanted to economize, stylize their lives in the American pattern; that is, to shape lives which were economical, casual, foreshortened, and to the point. They wanted to be less polite, and more genuine.

Spreading music across the empty countryside, the Edsel hurtled into the Dead Sea Valley, mile after mile down the great raw wall of the valley until we were at sea level, which was invisible, just a number, a theory, here; we sped on and down into the deepest hole on earth, until we reached the white, blinding floor of the valley, thirteen hundred feet below sea level. The heat had steadily increased from uncomfortable to the brink of intolerable. Heat crowded into the car like six extra passengers, poured past the windows like a steam bath. We drove across the wide empty valley—a white world of mounds and minarets of salt—through the thick still atmosphere, which seemed to have filtered up from the inner core of the earth, bits of scrub trying to grow here and there amid all the killing white mountains of salt. Off to the right in the distance were the green spearlike trees of the Jericho oasis, and on the left, looking much more presentable than its name, was the Dead Sea, serene, expansive, green-blue in the sunshine, its banks empty except for one large square building in the foreground, a hotel, and many miles away ahead of us the other wall of the valley rose, the worn-out red cliffs of the mountains of Moab.

We came to a bridge over a little green stream: the River Jordan. There was a police checkpoint there, and one of the policemen, in khaki uniform and pith helmet, looked at my passport, then at me, and then ordered me out of the car.

Had I done it again somehow, gotten into trouble with the police? There on the floor of the Dead Sea Valley it was an even more uncomfortable sensation than in London. Indecent exposure couldn't be it. Had the All-Purpose Spy reported me for something?

If so, he had gone to the top. I was being taken out of the car because the King wanted to see me. I was familiar enough with the life here not to be surprised that His Majesty knew where to find me, although I had not mentioned to anybody that I was going to Jerusalem. Jordan was small: 37,000 square miles. It had a population of 1,700,000. About 500,000 of these were refugees from Palestine, living in camps. Many thousands more were Bedouin roaming in the desert. There were only 40,000 people living in Amman, the capital. Like Lebanon, Jordan was a country where you could see almost everybody in it if you found just the right place to stand. King Hussein, hopping from appointment to appointment by helicopter, had come very close to finding the place.

I was driven back up from the white glare of the Dead Sea Valley in the first car going toward Amman, which the police stopped and put me into, back up to temperate Amman, to the gates of Basman Palace. It was heavily guarded by soldiers wearing khaki uniforms and the red and white checked Army headdress, the *kaffiyeh,* a headcloth fringed with white tassels and swirled dramatically around their heads and shoulders. They thoroughly searched the car, including under the seats and the engine. I was surprised that they did not search me. In protecting anyone as often threatened as King Hussein I had not expected any exceptions. But they didn't; respect for the visitor, the guest.

I was driven through the gates of Basman Palace, up a short curving driveway between lawns and trees and gardens, a sure sign of privilege in parched Jordan, the rarity of rarities —in the Moslem religion paradise is rich in water and greenery —to the doors of the long, pale yellow stone palace.

Here King Hussein had been left sitting, entirely alone, by history, on a little hill in a little town which was not exactly anywhere, a place along the route between ancient Arabia and ancient Syria, reigning over an accident, the Hashemite Kingdom of Jordan. It was all that was left to those who had led the flamboyant Arab Revolt of 1916–1918, when it had seemed that Hussein's family, the Hashemites, led by his great-uncle Feisal and his grandfather Abdullah and their complicated friend Lawrence of Arabia, were going to conquer as the armies of Mohammed himself had conquered, and recreate the glories of Imperial Arabia. Instead of that great renewed empire, comprising modern Syria, Iraq, Lebanon, Jordan, Palestine, Arabia and who knows how much else besides, the Hashemite leaders were all dead, except Hussein, and all the provinces were lost, except Jordan.

The Turkish Empire, under which these countries had rotted since the disintegration of their own Arab Empire in the thirteenth century, had, it's true, been driven away. Hussein's family, as the direct descendants of Mohammed and hereditary guardians of Holy Mecca, had provided the leadership for this second emergence of the Arabs from the Arabian peninsula. Like Mohammed, they struck, under Lawrence, at Aqaba first, and from that victory they advanced northward, raiding and harrying the Turkish garrisons and lines of communication, until, cooperating with a British army under General Allenby, they seized the hub of the Near East, Damascus, in 1918. Two years later Feisal was declared King of Syria, and it seemed that with this second astonishing Arab wave history was going to repeat itself.

The decline of the Hashemites from that pinnacle is a long, webbed chronicle of foreign intrigue, selfishness, mistrust, betrayal and murder, involving the French, the British, the Arab trait of mutual suspicion, Zionism, Nasserism, oil, and would be a book in itself. Many have already been written. The end of it all was inside Basman Palace, young King Hussein, stubbornly hanging on to what he and his grandfather had preserved in spite of everything.

Within the palace doors there was very little pomp and ceremony. Hussein was spiritually and actually a product of the desert; the Hashemite dynasty came from the bare landscape of Arabia, where simplicity was the only conceivable style of life. The land was not capable of sustaining more until it produced the oil, and hence the Cadillacs and jet planes and air-conditioned palaces which regale its current rulers, the Saudis, who wrested Saudi Arabia from King Hussein's family in the 1920's. Simplicity was the rule in Amman. Inside the front doors there was a moderate-sized lobby leading to two large wooden doors, and behind them was King Hussein's office. In front of these were two Circassian guards, fair descendants of migrants from Russia, wearing long black coats and black Persian lamb afghans, high black boots, bands of cartridges across their chests, and long ornamental daggers. Weapons, along with camels, were as significant in Jordan as jewelry was in Manhattan. I had never spent so much time so close to Sten guns, never had so many rifles leaning nearby, so many holsters faintly squeaking, seen so many naked blades. Jordan was a weaponed society; it might be and often enough was shoeless, but always there were weapons. They were carried as symbols, for prestige, and also because Jordan was not a completely orderly society, just as they are carried by the youth of New York City for the same reason. The two Circassian guards stood with their hands resting on the hilts of their daggers as Colonel Yasim, the Chief of Royal Protocol, led me into a waiting room, full of huge, gold-colored chairs. I sat down in one so large that I felt myself disappear. Colonel Yasim sat down at his desk next to me. He had a pleasant, sensible face, and wore a dark blue business suit. He was new at protocol, and certainly I was, so that neither of us was completely sure what we should do next. He scanned lists, and we both waited, and waited, and waited. "Protocol," I began to suspect, was a diplomatic word for "waiting." Noon came and went; hunger grew and grew. A Negro in red and black robes entered carrying a brass coffeepot with a curving spout; he gave me a little handleless cup and filled it with bitter, black, Bedouin coffee, good, tough, unsweetened coffee, the staff of life of the desert people. I started to hand him back the cup; he refilled it; I drank more—it is an insult to refuse a cup of coffee in Jordan—and this time remembered to shake the cup as I handed it back, which is the sole correct means to stop the flood. Then I waited some more. Later a soldier came in and gave me some heavily sugared tea. I continued to wait. An overwhelming Negro in a black robe rolled like a tower into the little room, bellowed greetings in Arabic, and rolled out again. He was an old man, although he didn't look it, who had come out of the Arabian desert with King Hussein's grandfather during the Revolt. A Pakistani holy man in a saffron robe drifted through; he had stopped off on his way back from making the pilgrimage to Mecca and not gotten any farther.

Then the telephone of the Chief of Royal Protocol rang. Colonel Yasim snatched it. *"Nam, sidi . . . nam, sidi . . . nam, sidi"* Yes, sir . . . yes, sir . . . yes, sir. King Hussein was setting the government of Jordan into motion for the day.

I was then led, rushed, into the King's office. It was apparent that the royal patience was short; the royal time, not a second of it, was to be wasted.

Hussein was sitting at a large, polished wooden desk to the right of the doorway, wearing a double-breasted business suit, beneath a large oil portrait of his grandfather, King Abdullah. He rose, smiling, and rapidly circled the desk as I came in, to shake hands. He was short and square, with a large head, long black mustache over his wide mouth, deeply set dark eyes. I saw him in many circumstances after that—issuing orders, confronting murderers, consoling a woman whose husband was near death, a son whose father had been assassinated—and these large deep-set dark eyes took on an extraordinary range of expressions; strong expressions of sincerity, nobility, compassion came easily to his eyes and face, and so did extreme impatience, utter determination and, when he looked at his wife, plain artless love.

His feelings seemed to be far more powerful than anything

else in him, and the only force which came close to equalling them was his will. In mental effort he tended to be a "plugger," doggedly mastering the necessary material. And the fourth quality of his nature which everyone noticed was his capacity for fast, audacious and irrevocable decisions. These qualities had kept him on the little perch where history had placed him for ten years, in spite of an array of plots, enmities, mutinies and handicaps which had a Perils-of-Pauline repetitiousness about them, one cliff-hanger a year at least, every episode guaranteed a thriller. If the Army wasn't being duped by his best friend into marching on his palace, then his private plane was being attacked without warning by jet fighters; if the Communists weren't trying to subvert him, the Nasserites were; if the Israeli frontier was calm, the Iraqi one burst into flame; if the latest plot to shoot him failed, they got his prime minister instead.

And beneath the unique tensions of King Hussein's life lay a family record of schizophrenia, which finally forced his father out of public life in 1952. King Hussein's younger brother, Prince Mohammed, had nervous problems. The family line seemed to be overbred: Hussein's ancestors, the Hashemites, descendants of the Prophet, had married only other Hashemites for many hundreds of years. As he greeted me with the natural charm of the family I asked myself how much additional will he had needed, and how much additional anguish he might have had to stand in his perilous life, because of the high-tension nerves inherited, along with a throne, from his family.

He turned and introduced me to another, younger brother, Prince Hassan, who was about to enter Harrow School in England. The little Prince was stiffly buttoned into a dark suit, and he shook my hand with a completely sustained seriousness, a firm hold on the duty he had to fulfill. He wanted no nonsense out of me. Then he sat and watched carefully while the King and I talked. In just this way, Hussein, when he was fifteen years old, spent month after month in this room, following every move and word of his grandfather, King Abdullah, learning as much as possible before King Abdullah was shot to death the following year, a step or two ahead of Hussein, at the portals of the great Mosque of Omar, in Jerusalem.

The King went to an armchair and indicated for me to sit on the couch at right angles. He did not sit any way; he sat straight and turned toward me, his arms along the armrests, and his feet flat on the floor and pointed straight ahead, one in front of the other. In Arab countries it is rude to show the sole of your shoe to anyone.

He was seeing me because I was living in Jordan, was interested in it, and was a writer. The King apparently saw, and had to see, almost everybody who had any dealings with Jordan. Not much work could be delegated, because too often the people who were competent weren't loyal, and the people who were loyal weren't competent. Hussein had to do most of it himself. That was another reason I had been hustled so quickly into his office; forty or so other people were waiting in rooms outside to see him.

He told me about his plans for Jordan, and then he described some of his closer brushes with death, and the economic hopes and problems of the country, and the happiness of his marriage that had at last broken the scarifying loneliness of his life. And then he invited me to go into the desert the next morning to see an artillery exercise. As I was going out the door four robed Bedouin were being rushed toward it.

The next morning at seven one of the black palace cars, not an Edsel but a Mercury, came for me at the Philadelphia. A soldier was at the wheel, and I joined Colonel Yasim in the back seat. He was wearing a dark suit and a white silk *kaffiyeh.*

We set out on the road going north from Amman. We talked about the Jordan Arab Army, formerly the Arab Legion under Glubb Pasha, who had been the second most powerful man in Jordan, and many said the first. It was this possibility which caused King Hussein to fire him and order him out of the country overnight in 1954.

For a young man in Jordan to be allowed to join the Army was a privilege. It represented modernity in an almost biblical land, power amid weakness, order in a rather feckless society, education, skills, a better life, prestige. It supported the state, as indispensably as the center pole in a tent.

In that sense Jordan was a military state, and there were advantages in that. The Army stood for order, for discipline, for masculine self-respect. Living in military Jordan helped me understand civilian France and the disdain the French Army has felt for the corruptions and confusions of the French Republics. In Jordan the Army firmly disciplined the chaotic urges of the people.

Everything in Jordan seemed small—the donkeys, the towns, the horses, the rivers, the trees, the incomes, the King—except the land itself, which was on the heroic scale: the enormous Dead Sea Valley had been my first sight of that. Here was my second: we turned off the northbound road and bounced off into the desert itself.

Everything in the desert seemed thin—the Bedouin, the camels, the dogs, the tents, the diets—except our car, which gradually seemed to inflate into a vast, swaying barge rolling ponderously across the sand. Hills the color of worn canvas undulated on all sides of us, and the horizon was a sharp line in the desert clarity, cut against the sky; the sky shone dramatically in different shades of blue, as though there were footlights out of sight beyond the hills. Millions of stones were scattered over the dead earth, and a peculiar feeling began to creep over me; there was of course no road or even a track, and as the car lurched into a dead, dusty saucer of ground, and the eight o'clock sun beat swelteringly down into it, the complete lifelessness became more and more inhospitable; the desolation outside was reflected inside me. There was not one thing to sustain us here except the internal combustion engine of the car, which was not infallible. If the car had been a horse or a camel it would have been more reassuring, we would have had at least one natural force working for us, but instead there was only this metal contrivance from Detroit, which was meant for roads. I had never realized before how metal a metal car was, never fully sensed the strangeness and foreignness of steel until I found myself inside it under that sun; its close resemblance to a furnace could be strongly felt, and also I felt that any minute one of the fenders might begin to slowly lengthen in the heat, that something was fundamentally wrong, as though the smallest fin on a fish you are about to eat faintly moved.

Then the Mercury pulled itself out of the dusty saucer and struggled up onto a flat plain where I could now see a half dozen cars and jeeps boiling along parallel with each other over the flatness, spumes of dust whirling up behind them, making for another cloud of dust in the distance.

Reaching that finally, we found two temporary wooden stands with burlap roofs filled with Jordanian officers in khaki uniforms and white and red checked *kaffiyeh,* or else berets, or garrison caps, Sten guns everywhere of course, and two artillery pieces on the desert floor in front of and below us. A few British officers were also quietly present, for although Glubb Pasha was gone the British influence on the Jordan Army was not.

It was remarkably hot. I had ignorantly come into the desert without a hat, the only person there without one, of course. The King's brother, Prince Mohammed, who was in his early twenties, stood chatting with a circle of officers, a slight figure looking theatrical in a khaki general's uniform, dark glasses, dapper black mustache, swagger stick and blue beret, but when I was taken up to him by Colonel Yasim the matinee-military look disappeared; an unaffected, cheery young man became visible past the dark glasses and swagger stick, speaking to me in an odd falsetto voice—a physical affliction he suffered from—welcoming me to Jordan with the family cordiality, and pausing now and then as some officer hastened up to him, seized his hands and fervently kissed them. As they straightened up again, the Prince knew how to look at them; his face expressed a mixture of gratitude at this act of loyalty to the throne, and humility about himself as a person.

Prince Mohammed, like his brother, had charm, a quality not much admired these days. Who cares about anything so superficial in the Atomic Age? Their father, the tormented Talal, also had charm in his own withdrawn way. Their grandfather, old King Abdullah, radiated it. Their great-uncle, King Feisal of Iraq, hypnotized everyone from Lawrence of Arabia and Gertrude Bell to the simplest Bedouin with a nostalgic, aquiline charm. The great-grandfather, Sherif Hussein of Mecca, was an extremely beguiling old party, those who met him reported, and so on, doubtless back to Mohammed the Prophet, whose magnetism was legendary.

But in meeting this family famous for its charm I began to think that it wasn't such a superficial quality after all. Watching them, it seemed that the charm sprang from a sense of measure and perspective they had about themselves, a humorous awareness of their limitations, a sense of proportion, a just self-perspective, and so, a streak of wisdom.

The morning sun rained down on us and on everything, and the customary royal wait for the arrival of King Hussein commenced. The prime minister who had been blown up the year before had been the only person in Jordan who had

had the self-confidence to wake King Hussein up in the morning, so that now the royal court spent a lot of time protocolling. Arabs are known for their fatalism and vagueness about time, but these officers didn't seem to be, as time melted away in the desert. I myself couldn't decide whether it was hotter to stand hatless in the open, or be in the shade under the burlap, where there was no ghost of air moving.

Finally he came, beating up toward us in a helicopter, rattled noisily overhead, and then, as every military man there snapped a salute, the helicopter settled to earth and all of the officers disappeared saluting into a storm of dust. When it cleared King Hussein could be seen striding smartly toward a small stand in front of the other two, followed by Prince Hassan.

The artillery exercise, like the appointments in his office, hurried to start the instant he sat down.

The King was not to be kept waiting; that was the iron law of the court which I accidentally broke a few hours later. King Hussein was receiving everyone in the Officers' Club, all forming a line to shake his hand, but having talked with the King the day before and not having any official status I thought I was not supposed to take part, until out of the corner of my eye I saw the last officer moving away from King Hussein and the Chief of Royal Protocol urgently waving to me. I was easily thirty yards away at the other end of the hall, and short of breaking into a run, there was nothing to do except walk as fast as possible through the court and high officers and the diplomatic corps of Jordan, all watching, while King Hussein protocolled, perhaps for the first time in his reign, until I made it to his presence and received a tight, brief, Hashemite smile.

King Hussein was often brusque, out of nervousness, a certain shyness, and most of all a deep physical craving for speed. He could not stand dawdling. The happiest moments of his life were spent thousands of feet in space flying jet fighter planes; on earth he had to be content with driving racing cars at top speeds. In conversation he charged, views and opinions and orders issuing like bullets. Procrastination, hesitation, indecision, equivocation, temporizing, all the dragging tactics of government officials everywhere were his enemies. Decide, act, order, start, do, finish, get there, leave, strike, attack: these were the qualities which relieved his tensions.

He sat with external patience through the artillery exercise. Batteries seven miles away laid down a smoke screen below us, medium field guns hit moving targets, all done with the calm precision of solving problems in geometry, and the officers sat murmuring technicalities to one another until it was over. Hussein and Hassan leaped into a jeep, raced down to congratulate the gun crews, sped up again, jumped into the helicopter and rattled away.

The rest of us got into our cars and jeeps and trucks and started out on another "shorter" route back to greenery and water and survival, and all the other vehicles quickly disappeared into their clouds of dust in other directions and we were soon alone again with only the Mercury. The yellow sand was looser in this part of the desert, and in order to keep from bathing in it we tightly closed all the windows. It could be seen swirling up along the panes, like water. Inside the car it was of course spectacularly hot. In spite of having everything closed, sand enfiladed up through the floor, and through other edges and cracks. Colonel Yasim's face became yellow with it, and, looking down, I saw that every tiny wrinkle of my pants was outlined by sand so that it looked like a relief map. My hair and eyelashes and face were also yellow. Bits of sand ground in my mouth. Then the driver turned around and with a gay smile said that he was lost.

The desert here was ridged and parched and empty, irregular with mounds and valleys and changes of texture. Suddenly I saw a sign of life, a robed man not too far away leading a donkey with a robed woman sitting on it, and she seemed to be holding something. The eerie Jesus-Mary-Joseph hallucinatory shock of it for a second convinced me that I had gone suddenly and completely crazy.

Then Colonel Yasim, Moslem to the core, broke the tension for me by seeing them too. "Some Bedouin," he said, but not the right kind of Bedouin, apparently, to ask for directions. The Mercury lurched over a ridge and we were alone again, stifling and sanded, boiling hot, hungry and lost.

Finally in a little sand valley we saw some black tents, which meant Bedouin who knew the region. They waved the direction to us, and before long we came to a "road sign," a little metal disc which seemed to mean a lot to the driver, and at last we saw a thin strip of green in the distance, which stood for life.

King Hussein next invited me to the settling of a blood feud.

These invitations were certainly more original than garden parties or yachting regattas or trooping of the colors or whatever royalty in the West had to offer. Not having taken a hat into the desert, I wondered if not taking a gun to this was equally foolish. Everyone would have a gun except me. It was the usual problem at royal courts: how to dress. I didn't have one and couldn't get one, and so as far as the four thousand Bedouin there were concerned, I didn't exist.

And there, on a huge and windy plain near the stronghold of Karak, with bands of Bedouin hurrying by shouting and racing each other on camels, all of them robed and hung with cartridge belts and knives, and a long black tent open on one side and filled with Bedouin chiefs and Moslem church leaders fingering their beads, and soldiers fondling their Sten guns, banners snapping, cushions, the All-Purpose Spy peering balefully from behind a tent flap, we all waited once more for King Hussein.

He was coming to force peace between two Bedouin tribes that had been killing each other. Mohammed was supposed to have accomplished this by uniting all Arabs under the flying banner of Islam, to have eliminated the bare justice of a life for a life as he had found it in Mecca and Medina, but here it still was, thirteen centuries later. Roaming through this immemorial scene of desert life I felt something rekindled in myself, a faint wave of impatience at not having a gun and not understanding what they were all thinking, of themselves, of one another, of me. Something I couldn't identify began to stir in me as the cries of the Bedouin grew wilder, and the realization struck me that after all, half these four thousand armed men were mortal enemies of the other half, and that this was quite a nervous tense mob around me.

Just then I saw a flash of pink amid the prevailing browns and whites and blacks and khakis. A pink dress; it was a girl of about twenty, alone, walking through the swirl of over-excited warriors, the only woman anywhere for great distances. She came nonchalantly along and went up to the first officer who crossed her path; he happened to be the Commander-in-Chief of the Army. "Hello," she said brightly. "When's Hussein getting here?"

The Commander-in-Chief looked dazed for a moment, rallied, and smiling gently, said, "His Majesty King Hussein will arrive soon. And you, please, who are you?"

"My name is Sally Potter. I was just driving by," she waved vaguely at the distant road. There was a Volkswagen parked on it, and standing beside it was a young man, apparently an American too. "And I saw all these people and flags and I thought it must be something that Hussein would be at. I really want to see him. My friend Petie and I are driving to Petra, but this looked like a good chance to stop and see Hussein if he's going to be here."

Bedouin are self-centered, proud people, and they had not deigned to notice anything as unrelated to themselves as Sally at first. Now, however, they were becoming aware of her, and many pairs of black eyes were glaring unblinkingly at her.

The Commander-in-Chief then began talking calmly and reassuringly to her, as you would to a horse who hadn't noticed that the barn was on fire, talking and slowly leading her unemphatically back through the four thousand excited Bedouin men toward her Volkswagen and her way of life.

She reached the automobile safely, and was persuaded to drive on to Petra without waiting to see the King arbitrate a blood feud on which his throne might depend. She thought of this vital confrontation as if it were a tourist attraction, the Changing of the Guard at Buckingham Palace.

And her American assertiveness, wading along between two armed camps, was it to be admired or not?

One thing could be said positively: it was certainly different from anything women here were capable of. In Jordan the women were still mostly veiled and all but invisible. In some of the homes I was invited to they were not so much as glimpsed between the curtains, and food and drink seemed to have prepared themselves. In others the women could be sensed if not exactly seen, just behind the curtains. And sometimes I was finally even allowed to meet them, in awkward circumstances, standing in the hallway, or on the stairs. They were incarcerated, and it was clear that the men, at least, liked it that way, being free to sit untroubled over their coffee and bubble pipes in the cafés, or if they were sophisticated and "Westernized," ordering bottles of Scotch in the arid nightclub of the Philadelphia and making passes at the foreign girls in the floor show.

And what about Petie, the American male, back at the car? He apparently hadn't thought venturing into this wild scene a very good idea, had tried to dissuade Sally, failed, and let her go, and let her go alone. Amid this crowd of domineering warriors Petie's brand of maleness was pathetic in its passivity.

I remembered gatherings of middle-aged couples in America, where the men sat back, slowly turning their cigars in their mouths while the women talked uninterruptedly for them to each other. Slower-thinking, lazier, less socially alert, the men let their wives take over. The reversal from the age-old way of life here was complete.

Which was better? Half the answer was clear: the man-dominated way of life here was far better, for men. It was not so clear whether the freer, more assertive, emancipated life women lead in America was better for women. It was their right, of course, and yes, women must have full opportunities to fulfill themselves and develop and evolve and express themselves, and yes, many Arab women were wretchedly downtrodden in this patriarchal world of warriors; but yes, also, there was a firmness here to the image of what a woman was and what a man was which had become blurred in America, and yes, also, women here were more at peace with themselves.

But it was the American man who seemed worst off of all, when looked at from the point of view of the unquestioned masculine authority of the desert. The economic bigness of the United States, merging into bigger and ever bigger entities, gave American men jobs in organizations of many thousands of other men, where assertiveness, independence and aggressiveness tended to be more liabilities than assets; the assets were cooperativeness, malleability, and guile, all traditionally feminine traits. It wasn't surprising that at home he could not transform himself into a pillar of male authority, but tended to be inactive most of the time, punctuated by occasional violent explosions.

Sally and Petie, with Sally at the wheel, drove on to Petra, and a little later King Hussein finally arrived. He came across the plain, standing in the rear of an open automobile and frantic shouting greeted his progress, camels circled nervously as their riders cried out, uproar mounted on uproar, everybody pressed forward closer and closer toward the King. The Bedouin were easily his most loyal subjects. A great many of the townspeople in Jordan felt drawn strongly to dissolve Jordan and join President Nasser's United Arab Republic, and the half-a-million refugees from Palestine were generally alienated. But these desert Arabs here knew that he was the tribal chief of chiefs, and their acclaim sounded much more genuine than any I had heard for the King anywhere else.

Hussein got out of the car and took his place in the middle of the long narrow open tent. I happened to be standing nearby, and was immediately engulfed by shouting Bedouin. It was the next thing to a riot, and no one was calm or still except the King, standing motionless and faintly smiling in the vortex. The soldiers were engulfed along with everybody else, but the strange thing was that for the first time in Jordan I felt trust in the air, the most threatened monarch in the world seemed to feel safe and to be safe here at the heart of his desert people, and the Army, which closely scrutinized everything that came anywhere near his person in Amman, fell back philosophically here and let this armed-to-the-teeth mob embrace him. Hussein's face was unreadable in its faintly smiling calmness, but I believed that he could only be quietly happy. The loyalty to him here seemed so obvious and so heartfelt; it was the sort of powerful, genuine acclaim youth gives the people it admires: the sense of fidelity here was young. After the snake pit of treachery where he usually lived, this had to be a moment of deep satisfaction.

Then he got down to the business at hand, which was death. We all sat down on cushions, and I found to my surprise that one of the high officers of the Army had maneuvered me into the circle of six or eight people who were to settle this desert blood feud.

Now I felt not so much foreign as in a dream, the bad kind of dream where you find yourself about to address Congress on a subject everybody knows except you, or at the controls of a space capsule. King Hussein began slowly speaking in Arabic to the Commander-in-Chief of the Army, who sat on his left, and a handsome fifteen-year-old boy, named Amjad Majali, in a black robe and white *kaffiyeh,* sitting on his right. The feud had started when the boy's father, Prime Minister Majali, had been assassinated by means of a bomb planted in his desk. The Prime Minister had been an extremely likable man, according to everyone; later I was allowed to read his diary, and it was a disarmingly direct tale of a fairly wild and irresponsible desert boy who eventually pulled himself together, got his education and succeeded brilliantly. Then, of course, at the peak of his career, came death at the hands of a member of another desert tribe, the Tahers.

Five of them came slowly straggling toward us now, two in Bedouin robes, two in Western clothes, and one in both. The Bedouin massed in front of us fell back and cleared a corridor for them, and the most striking thing of all was that a perfect silence now fell over the mob. The five of them came slowly on and began taking the hands of the two Majalis, not speaking or being spoken to, and one of the Tahers, a broken-looking bearded old man in white robes, slowly leaned forward and kissed Amjad Majali on the cheek. The boy seemed just able to bear that.

Then we all sat down in a circle and King Hussein began slowly speaking to them, telling them that they must bury their differences and all work together as one Arab people, speaking slowly for about ten minutes in that vein, carrying on the message, that is, of his ancestor the Prophet, who had urged this same reconciliation on the feuding people of Medina, had succeeded in that, and so started the Arabs on their abrupt achievement of world power.

Then those of us in the circle were given ceremonial Bedouin coffee. I was still in a dilemma, without any idea of why I had been included or what I ought to do or not do, fearful that I might violate some fundamental of the elaborate courtesies which were mortally important on this occasion.

After that, I believe I signed the peace document. Then there was a banquet, called a *mansef,* which followed in a vast adjoining tent. Down the long table there was platter after platter of whole roast lamb, all of the lamb—hooves, head held up straight, teeth, everything—sitting in a sea of rice. We formed around a platter, ripped a piece off the carcass, rolled it in rice and snapped it into our mouths. A middle-aged sheikh across the table from me tossed choice bits of lamb he unearthed over to me as a sign of hospitality. They were good.

So, over platters of lamb and rice, the blood feud ended. Justice had been imposed; four men had died, two from each family. A life for a life; it must be the most ancient attempt at justice in the world, and also the most ancient form of "police force," each family being its own vigilantes.

It was, after all, justice of a very direct and, in its own terms, equitable kind, I was not sure that the legal maze we had in America was any real improvement, since part of the legal code was benighted, some of the police and judges were corrupt, and almost everything was very slow and very expensive. Especially in view of the Kafka legal cesspool which had nearly engulfed me in London, I felt it might be better to face justice from the Bedouin.

Then it was over and we all started north on the straight road back to Amman in cars, on motorcycles or on camels. Some of the camels stopped to scratch their necks against telephone poles, just as at the camel races in Amman some would stop to chew a weed along the course. A flash of red cloth, a solitary soldier's headdress, on rocks overlooking the road, showed that the Army was guarding the royal route. Children were gathered at villages to cheer the King, and families sat in a row in front of their huts to watch. The flat highland north of Karak abruptly ended in a huge gray canyon, and then squirmed up the other side. The vastness of the land itself was once again imposed, hugeness asserted its fundamental and silent presence, overawing, the unbudgeable fact of the Near East. The people scratch the surface here and there, put up little contrivances like the Damascus Mosque, but can make no real impression on the overpowering natural facts which dominate their lives. Arabs are fatalists. Facing this forbidding vastness with only a camel and a tent, who wouldn't be?

As suddenly as the royal invitations had started, they stopped. Colonel Yasim was never in when I called him, and he never called me again. It was a normal experience at oriental courts, dropping suddenly and inexplicably out of favor. At least, unlike Colonel Ramayah, I was not going to be arrested.

What had I done? Nothing probably, I was just Out of Favor, or forgotten. This would not have mattered, since I wasn't running for office in Jordan, except that I had been given to understand that I should be available whenever the King wanted to see me. My experience in being stopped halfway to Jerusalem and brought back showed how literally this was meant. I was supposed to be available at the Philadelphia Hotel, I was not to keep the King waiting again. So I spent a lot of time beside the tepid swimming pool, or reading. I recalled what the famous young Frenchman had said to me: "You're going to be bored . . . bored. . . ." How had he been so sure, and so right? The boredom and inertia of Asia lowered itself over me: wait. I spent a lot of time listening torpidly while the intrigues of the Near East were discussed, rumors of smuggling, gun-running, Army mutinies, risings, snipings, bribery, spies, high-level love affairs. There were also constructive rumors, sometimes, about new plans to irrigate the Dead Sea Valley, to resettle the refugees, open new schools, start new industries.

I had no part in any of this, and inaction began to drain my energy away. I took to napping in the afternoon more and more. Awake, I spent a lot of time watching a workman diligently employed in the restoration of the Roman amphitheater across from the hotel. In his voluminous white work cloths and *kaffiyeh,* he would sit cross-legged Arab-style in front of a huge cube of beautiful white native stone, in a faint haze of stone dust, hammering musically on the block. A square of burlap on a wooden stick which was planted in the ground near him, looking like a boat sail, threw a patch of shade over him. His musical ping-ping never seemed to flag, on and on hour after hour it went steadily, except when the call to prayer sailed down from the minaret through the canyons of Amman. Then he would lay aside his hammer and chisel, kneel on a little rug facing Mecca, not far to the south, touch his forehead to the ground, then sit back on his heels for a while, then prostrate himself again, and then finally return to his stone and the steady music of his diligent chisel work. I thought he seemed a contented man, and as my days dragged on, an enviable man.

The landscape of Jordan is practically all rock, gray on the surface, a beautiful white just underneath which, when cut into, reveals a glowing pink interior, as though Jordan were a human body turned to stone. And all over its populated parts this same busy musical pinging of chisels was the characteristic sound of the country, the music of a slow, hard and permanent work of renewed construction.

Jordan is a land made of rock. The desert is either rock itself or dissolved rock, sand. The great mountains and cliffs are rocks; everything man makes there is made with stone.

Day followed day in cloudless Amman. Inaction was becoming habitual with me. Once in a while I went to a party given by people at the American Embassy. One day a revolution happened across the border in Syria, and I turned what attention I could muster on that; it didn't look as though it were going to be much of a revolution. However, King Hussein was rumored to be very excited, and suddenly the flying correspondents and photographers for *Life* and *Paris Match* were in Amman, strapped into camera harness, worked up, on the go; one of them was a parachutist who had planned to float down on revolting Damascus. Every day the spies and I saw them off from the Philadelphia porch to the Syrian frontier, and every evening we welcomed them back, barred from crossing the border. Finally one day they didn't come back, and Amman settled down into inaction again.

Sitting around like this was not supposed to be an American talent. I couldn't say that I was enjoying it, but I was learning to tolerate it and then live with it and then not mind it particularly, and I was not at all tempted to run to the fire in Syria with the other boys. I was losing my grip.

I took aimless walks all through Amman, up the dry, pebbly riverbed running through the center of town, where a ramshackle bazaar had been set up under tents; through a little back street full of little shops selling little pieces of silver jewelry; to the mosque, where I took off my shoes and was ardently welcomed by a plump hurrying Aladdin of a man—"Welcome to my mosque!"—who then went padding importantly off again; up to a tiny version of the Taj Mahal on top of one of Amman's seven hills, the mausoleum of King Hussein's assassinated grandfather, King Abdullah, a pretty but neglected-looking place despite the sentinel on duty, with the sarcophagus and a copy of the Koran visible within; to the airport to watch, from a distance, the King and his circle race Go-Karts, with a royal victory always the outcome; to incomprehensible movies; to the one nightclub in town, which while lively and even a little sinister, suffered from the complete absence of women; and I went here and there and nowhere in particular, wandering alone around this town in the Mesopotamian desert—and the musky smell of it, the pale blue sky, the light gray cast of the place generally, these impressions in their complete foreignness coaxed me into a state of vague and passive inaction. It didn't matter what I did or didn't do in a place so unrelated to my life; certainly nobody in Jordan cared. I had exactly one imperative to live by: DON'T KEEP KING HUSSEIN WAITING, and now I no longer had access to the royal presence so even that duty had lapsed. A value of travel, that is real travel in far distant places, was happening to me. At home life was aggravating because the aggravation was always, always the same. Here old anxieties were given a long-needed rest; new ones broke out in all their novelty. Appointments, commitments, engagements, deadlines had hounded me for a long time in the United States; here, I had nothing whatever to do. On the other hand, at home I lived in the happy anonymity of the crowded Northeast, and did what I wanted without worrying; here, I was being watched, in a routine way. That was an irritation, but a stimulating one in its strangeness. At home, my mind was glutted and sick with the plethora of things being hawked and displayed and owned and thrown away; here, there were the Edsels, and that was about all in the line of things. In such a strange country the pressures of years are relieved, new ones are applied, and you begin to change.

Nothing to do, nowhere to go, nothing to talk about, the same simple meals, the same faces, same weather, this continued until one day I suddenly realized that after all I was free to go; the prison door had been unlocked all the time, King Hussein had talked to me and taken me here and there and been very kind to me, and that was that. There had been some discussion of my writing a book about his life; but one day as he was leaving a function by helicopter sheafs of paper escaped from the cabin and sailed down on the senior officers of his Army, who went scrambling for them, struggling for possession with a group of excited schoolchildren, and when I happened to ask what the pages were, someone brightly informed me that this was the King's autobiography, which he was completing just then with the help of the English journalist Noel Barber, and I then decided unilaterally that my particular project was out.

The movie director David Lean turned up at the Philadelphia. Somewhere in the dead valleys of south Jordan he was filming the life of Lawrence of Arabia. I had been asked to visit the company there, but the royal prerogative had held me back; now they had only one more day of work in Jordan left, and I decided to go.

We left in a small, two-engined plane from Amman Airport early in the morning and flew south. The great east-west valley I had crossed by car the day of the blood-feud peace-parley spread itself below; it could be seen from here to widen magnificently as it went westward, ending in the Dead Sea, a long bluish haze on the far right below. We passed over the long, smooth Karak plateau, and then the land suddenly dropped away into broken hills and strange valleys. Now rusty-iron mountains cut across the land east to west, and gradually an unearthly, sand-colored, flat, vague, cloudlike desert emerged below us, with encrusted iron-red mountains sticking singly up from it, a moonscape, tremendous reeflike ridges rising as if from a flat, sand-colored sea; the desert and the rock mountains below acquired a reddish, hellish cast from the morning sun. There was not a single scratch of man's presence visible anywhere; it all looked much too clean to be real, the red mountains throwing long, black, jagged shadows on the vague and cloudy crimson of the desert floor.

We began to come down; below now was a vast corridor of sand between two huge walls of rock—Wadi Rumm. I at last noticed something suggesting human beings, something other than rock and sand, a flash of silver: it was another plane, on the ground. I also saw a tent or two, and then our plane was coming in for a landing on the rock-hard desert. Soon we stepped out of the plane into the spun-crystal clearness of morning in the desert. In the distance a large sheet of "water" was reflecting the mountains behind it. This was the local mirage, working as usual.

With the plane's motors turned off, a windless silence demonstrated that there had never been anything as loud as an airplane here before, that this was a preserve which the fumes of Western civilization hadn't penetrated until now, a place of indeterminate perspectives, interminable silences and unflawed clarity. Even this huge film operation with its airplanes and fleets of vehicles and hoards of extras and animals was swallowed up and muffled and lost like a tribe of ants in all the silence and space.

Jeep engines erupted defiantly into the quietness, and we set off to drive from where the airplane had landed ten spine-shaking miles into Wadi Rumm, up a bumpy track through sand which now seemed striped in shades of pink and yellow and green, up to a group of frail tents and wooden stables. Members of the Jordan Army cavalry who were being used in the film lived in the tents; their horses had more solid accommodations in the stables. The jeeps continued over a rise and past more tents scattered with less order over the dunes; the Bedouin lived here with their camels and provided entirely authentic extras for the movie, playing their own fathers and grandfathers who had served with Lawrence during the Arab Revolt.

The jeeps lurched on, driving past a small, neat stone fort enclosed by barbed wire. A tall Arab in khaki-colored blouse and skirt reaching to his ankles, cartridge belts across his chest, head swathed in the Arab headdress, stood near the fort.

"That'll photograph well," I remarked, "but with the naked eye you can see that it's too perfect to be real."

"That is real. That's a Jordan Desert Patrol outpost."

Oh.

Finally, several dusty miles later, the group of jeeps reached an immense basin in the desert, at the foot of a gigantic rock cliff, where there was a little spray of huts and tents. This was the forward headquarters of the great film company.

The shooting location for this last day, however, was even further up the valley. The jeeps bumped and swerved on, over far rougher terrain since the track into the valley ended at the forward headquarters. They went rocking and pitching over and around big clumps of witch-camel grass, swerving and swaying like little speedboats in a heavy sea. After a couple of miles of this they arrived at a tiny commotion in the vastness, a little wrinkle on the great face of the wadi; the epic production-in-progress of *Lawrence of Arabia*.

Three bright little beach umbrellas shaded some camp chairs. There was a large camera truck and a large sound truck; there were jeeps. British technicians in shorts, with fair hair and blazing faces, loitered around the trucks; young Arab assistants in nondescript shirts and pants, but never shorts, idly chased lizards with sticks; European actors with dyed skin stood around in Bedouin robes; real dark Bedouin hovered in their own robes; an evil-faced Arab leaned down from his camel and said in clear Anglo-Saxon, "Eddie, it doesn't feel as though there's any foam rubber in this saddle to *me,*" and a figure in white hood and voluminous robes, also on the apex of a camel, began to lope off by himself. This was the movie's part-time Lawrence of Arabia: not the actor portraying Lawrence but the stand-in for that actor used for long shots. Like a mirror reflecting a reflection, this white figure swaying away on a camel began as it receded over the terrain Lawrence had known to embody Lawrence himself, to look more and more strange and alone and willful, all the actorish quality fading away as he sat swaying atop the steep pyramid which a camel seen from behind forms, a diminishing white figure loping toward a huge red slab of cliff alone.

This was the country he had roamed over and fought through; below us as we flew down here had been the Istanbul to Mecca Railroad, that he dynamited many times with such exuberance between 1916 and 1918, cutting the lines of communication of the Turkish Empire in the cause of Arab liberation and Allied victory. Later I saw the railroad from the ground; it was still the wreck Lawrence had left it. Later also I met an old sheikh who had known him during the Revolt: "A very clever man, Colonel Aurens, very clever." In many ways he was present in Jordan the whole time I was there, very much present despite a seemingly willful neglect of his memory; the Arabs did not seem to want much credit for the Arab victory over Turkey to go to this unclassifiable wraith from Oxford. His Arab comrades at the time had felt differently. One of them said in those days: "You ask why we love Lawrence? And who can help loving him? He is our brother, our friend, and leader. He is one of us, there is nothing we do he cannot do, and he even excels us in doing it. He takes such an interest in us and cares for our welfare. We respect him and greatly admire his courage and bravery: we love him because he loves us, and we would lay down our lives for him."

Now, a thousand intrigues later, it was different; but neglected or not, Lawrence was still very much present in Jordan. He was there in the wrecked railroad, in conversation, in recollection; he was there because he had not been laid to rest in people's minds, because they were still uneasy about him; it was not the ghost but the haunted who were restless. The Jordanians and the English, heirs to what Lawrence helped accomplish in liberating the land from Turkey, would not let him rest in peace. When he entered their minds, their brows knit, voices turned edgy or querulous or dubious, and they would say something ambivalent: "Oh, he was a *gifted* chap, all right!" or "Aurens? Yes, he helped us, oh yes, we admired what he did, yes." He remains controversial. I did not see any trace of a monument, or memorial, scroll, or plaque anywhere to recall his memory, which perhaps was not so much unpardonable neglect as uneasiness, as though his influence might be too potent if focused in some kind of memorial to him in Jordan.

Meanwhile his spirit in the most practical way possible was sweeping the country. This film, taken from his life and his book, *The Seven Pillars of Wisdom,* was pouring money and jobs into neglected Jordan. Lawrence always was contradictory, out of kilter, fumbling the simplest things and only succeeding at the impossible; it was entirely in character that, dead since 1935, his influence would now be turning Arab nomads into movie actors.

Part of the bafflement and impatience people still felt about Lawrence resulted from his behavior after 1918, when as the most flamboyantly famous hero of the world war he seemed destined to become a viceroy, or a cabinet minister, or at least a general. Instead he went through the ordeal of the Versailles Peace Conference, where the promises made to the Arabs were cut to pieces, wrote his account of the Revolt, and then began his mystifying retreat into the ranks of the Royal Air Force as an ordinary airman, steadily year by year, refusing every honor, every opportunity, every reward of his accomplishments and fame.

This renunciation isn't so mystifying now, now that he has been dead so long and so much has been published about his life. It seems clear now that beginning while the Revolt was still in progress, Lawrence experienced a series of "nervous breakdowns," a collapse of the ego, waves of loathing for his own grandeur and the blood he had swum through to achieve it that completely ate away the central strength of his character, his will. This will had overridden every shading and hesitation of a complicated and sensitive personality; and beginning in 1917 his outraged nature began to take revenge, reducing him to self-horror at what he had done, and a need for nothing but therapy, mechanical tasks to perform, orders to *follow,* never to give. So fastidious he did not like to be touched by others, he had nevertheless ordered and wallowed in bloodthirsty slaughters during the war. The will-less, ironclad routine of military life was all he felt safe in allowing himself after that, and it preserved him until his time in the Air Force expired in 1935. Soon afterward he records being driven wild by a mere bird persistently fluttering at his window, and soon after that, roaring through the countryside on his high-powered motorcycle, he was thrown and killed, leaving behind a feeling like an unresolved chord in music.

The man in white on the camel, the reflection of Lawrence's reflection, was now just a small moving spot at the bottom of the immense wall of Wadi Rumm, where he joined a large band of men on horses and camels.

David Lean remained back beside the camera truck. Until now he had been a very inconspicuous member of the group there, a tall, thin, middle-aged man with a sensitive, harried face, wearing loose tan slacks and a shortsleeved shirt. He now coiled himself tensely into a camp chair and began to fume. The band of men and animals a mile away weren't in the exact position he wanted. "Move column nearer to us!" an assistant director said through a hand loudspeaker. His augmented voice went out like a siren across the sand and camel grass, and much later it echoed faintly back from a cleft deep in the cliff. No one of the minute figures in the column seemed to hear. Again and again the direction shot out toward the cliff, bounced faintly back, and nothing happened. Finally a jeep was sent to tell them what to do. It clambered and lurched among the desert and grass, a vague whirl of dust rising from its back wheels, and at last it crept up to the column. After a while the column began to move into the position Lean wanted. But then, for some reason, the jeep did not withdraw. "Jeep, come back!" the assistant director bawled into his loudspeaker. Nothing happened. This new order sailed out across the wadi again and again; still nothing happened. David Lean climbed onto the roof of the camera truck, next to the camera itself, and kept repeating in his sharp Londoner's voice, "Get them out of there, tell them to come back."

At length the jeep began to make its slow, dusty way out of camera range. But Lean could not wait for its return. Once it was definitely out of range of the shot which was about to be made he ordered the assistant director to tell it to stop where it was, so that filming could begin. This third order went out across the sand quite a few times before it got through to the driver of the jeep, which jounced once more and then stopped, seeming to break down, to be stuck halfway between actors and camera for good.

"All right, everybody, quiet," said the assistant director into his loudspeaker.

"Shut up!" shouted David Lean without help. A complete but uneasy silence followed.

There were one or two professional clicks and snaps, and then an assistant fired a gun to signal to the troop of mounted men to begin the scene. They then set out, just perceptibly moving across in front of the huge dark red slab of rock, a little tribe of insects inching along beneath the great wall of the valley. Around the camera truck, Lean and the camera-men and the assistant directors and the script girl and some Jordanian helpers stood motionless. There was no sound to be heard except a little scratching noise coming from the sound truck and a little pennant attached to the camera truck which snapped now and then in the doubtful breeze. Inside the large camera next to Lean a few feet of film were being exposed.

In a minute or so it was finished. Most of the morning had been spent preparing for this scrap, but there was a little time left, so everyone hastened to pack up chairs and um-brellas, and then the two trucks and accompanying jeeps began working their way forward toward the cliff, for a close-up of the same shot.

David Lean began with the women in the scene. They were playing Bedouin wives and were dressed in black ac-cordingly, but they were not quite authentic. Bedouin women are not supposed to be photographed. So these city Arab women had been brought in from Jerusalem, and since they looked very much like the real thing they were the object of many doubts and suspicions on the part of the real

Bedouin men in the movie. They were arranged very interestingly, seated on top of a big rock outcrop.

But Lean was not entirely happy about their positioning. An Arab-speaking assistant went up onto the rock in the relentless sunshine, and Lean said through another assistant with a loudspeaker, "Will you ask the lady second from the right to move forward—yes, now back a little, just a bit, now will she sit down, no, the way she sat before, so that the red in her sleeves shows"—doubtfully—"y-e-e-s-s—and now will the other lady next to her. . . ."

For half an hour the women on the rock were rearranged, and the small army of men on camels and horseback were held in readiness below them on the floor of the valley.

Then at last this shot too was ready.

"Quiet, please, everybody quiet," said the loudspeaker.

"Shut up!" shouted Lean.

The gun was fired, and the large body of men on horses and camels started forward in a jumbled desert mass, the camels hung with blankets and tassels, their riders wearing their headcloths banditlike across their mouths to filter the dust, rifles slung on their backs, caparisoned horses hurrying along in the confusion and red dust, and slightly higher than anyone, Lawrence of Arabia, or so it seemed, a hooded white figure hunched forward on his pitching camel. Above them the women rose and came forward to the edge of the rock, ululating—the high Arab women's cry, a high steady note broken by blocking the mouth quickly over and over with the hand.

It was this last detail which failed. From lack of practice or shyness the women didn't ululate enough to satisfy David Lean. Back went the horses and camels, back to their original sitting position went the women on the rock, higher and hotter rose the sun. "Quiet please" and "Shut up!" broke the desert air again, and once more the camels and horses and riders and the women on the rock converged toward the camera and Lean.

This time it would do. The umbrellas and chairs were swept up, the jeeps started their engines, and everyone piled into them to drive two miles back to the forward headquarters for lunch. It was solid plain European food, dished out in a tent for everyone except the principal figures in the production, who were served in wooden huts.

Then everyone got into jeeps again and bounced back to the new location, a little deeper than before into Wadi Rumm. Now there was a really long wait.

This was to be the last scene made in Jordan. Everything was far behind schedule. Large sections of the huge script were still being rewritten; scenes were being rehearsed and re-rehearsed and shot and re-shot; a thousand details were slightly wrong; a thousand little snags were always developing; and above all there was the perfectionism of David Lean, which was turning *Lawrence of Arabia* into an unforeseen kind of epic. It looked as if it would cost more than the Arab Revolt itself had cost; it was certain to take longer to film than it had taken Lawrence and the Arabs to break the Turkish Empire. European members of the company, including Lean himself, had been hurrying into hospitals in Jerusalem and Amman lately with some sudden complaint or other. The pilot of one of the airplanes had come in for a landing a few days before with Anthony Quinn aboard and forgotten to lower his wheels. The desert was very smooth, so that only the plane had been damaged. Someone stole a large and valuable phonograph record collection out of Lean's trailer. It was established that none of the Arabs was guilty.

Morale was low. The British technicians, used to all the protections and privilege of a welfare state, complained steadily about rights which were being denied them. The Bedouin alone were comfortable, and accepted what came with steady desert resignation. But even they had their doubts. "They think we're balmy," said the actor Peter O'Toole succinctly, one of the few Europeans who made an attempt to get to know them. It was appropriate that he should: he was playing Lawrence.

That afternoon, preparations for the final scene, which was centered on him, went slowly forward. It was to be a very ambitious scene. The camera was set up on a medium-sized boulder and pointed toward the sun. In the foreground, on the boulder, O'Toole and two other actors were to play out the short scene. Behind them on a hillside sloping downward from left to right scores of camels were stationed, with their riders standing in front of them. And behind them there was the moonlike floor of Wadi Rumm stretching off toward the red-rock bastions of the far distant west ridge. It all looked extremely effective: Lawrence in a soiled British World War I belted summer uniform slumped exhausted on the rock; two desert sheikhs in their robes standing patriarchally over him; and on the hillside the high-legged, high-nosed camels with robes in deep colors flung over their humps, their riders on foot, in robes and headcloths, and underfoot small rocks—thousands of them—dark-colored rocks growing by the minute more dramatic as the declining sun threw little shadows beside them. And finally in the distance, the great desert valley was also passing into the shadow of its far cliffs.

But there were a number of things which did not please David Lean. First of all, and crucially, the camera was pointed toward the west, and had to be carefully angled so that the sun would not enter the lens and of course make photography itself impossible. The proper placement of it took much time; and when just the right position had at last been decided on, a shield perhaps a foot square had to be held above the lens by an assistant to make the shot possible. A rock outcrop near the parade of camels reflected too much light for Lean's taste, so a man was dispatched to spray it a darker shade.

And then, what about the dialogue? It consisted of only four or five lines, but how were they to be said? Should Peter O'Toole be seated on the rock throughout the scene, or should he enter walking and then sink down in exhaustion? Lean rehearsed O'Toole doing it both ways. The veteran English actor John Ruddock, playing one of the sheikhs, stood behind O'Toole. "This is the sun's anvil—" said Ruddock. But was standing the best position for him as he said this line? Lean had him sit. "This is the sun's anvil—" he said again. Perhaps he should begin by sitting and then stand up as he said the line. And the other sheikh, should he sit, stand or do both? The three actors were led by Lean to try it in all possible combinations—sitting, standing, two sitting and one standing, one sitting and two standing, one or more of them getting up or sitting down during the course of this minute scene. Which way was better, which way was best, which way was—for this was what Lean pursued and why it had to be tried in all possible fashions—perfect?

"Where did you get those awful boots?" he suddenly said to O'Toole.

"I've been wearing them right along," the young actor answered with a smirk.

"Got that one past me," muttered Lean.

Finally all the decisions about camera angle, reflectors, the rocks, the robes, the camels, the desert floor, the actors, their postures, the lines and how they were to be delivered had been reached. The scene was ready to be put on film. For some last-second attention to his makeup O'Toole moved a few steps away from the camera and sat down on a stool. His makeup man quickly sprayed some dust on his uniform and began giving him some extra sweat. David Lean suddenly loomed over him, muttering breathlessly, "Hurry up! Hurry up!" With his loose, light summer clothes flapping on his tall thin frame, he jerked across the rock, consciously clamping control on his nerves. "We haven't much time!" he said in this same electric undertone. "Hurry!"

O'Toole took a last look at his long, regular-featured, slightly wayward-looking, suntanned face in a mirror, at his bright yellow dyed hair, and stood up.

Absolute silence ensued; the scene began. At a signal the men with the camels began to move slowly down the hillside behind, and the deep reds and purples of their robes and the camels' caparisons made a striking procession against the rocky, shadowy hillside. O'Toole stepped in front of the camera and sank exhausted on the rock. Behind him, the sheikh began his line, "This is the sun's anvil—"

"Stop," said David Lean quietly. "I'm sorry, it's too late."

The sun at that moment had entered the camera. The scene was unfilmable.

O'Toole let fall a discouraged "Fuck." "I'm sorry," he said, "I'm sorry." Because his extra attention to his makeup had been the final delay, he seemed to conclude that the failure was due to him. He had forgotten that it was David Lean who had rehearsed the scene to the point where the slightest delay would be fatal.

The director stood amid the wrecked scene alone for a moment wearing the look of tense pleasure certain sensitive faces wear when confronting deep disappointment.

And then everything began to be folded and packed with the practical haste of, say, a group of Arab nomads, the camera and umbrellas and stools and kits, the paint, the light reflectors; into the trucks and jeeps it all went, followed by the technicians, the actors and the director. Like an army in disorderly retreat after a bad defeat they jounced and careened away down the desert valley, and not far behind them the Bedouin in their hundreds swayed along on their camels with much more composure. Few, if any, knew what had happened or why, nor could they be expected to care. They knew that they were going to get their final pay, that this unusual form of labor was over.

But for the *Lawrence of Arabia* company it was the end, on a very sour note, of filming in Jordan. The huge machinery which had brought and sustained them here was already well advanced in the process of carrying them out again, and could not be stopped for another attempt at the scene tomorrow. They bounced down Wadi Rumm and into the airplanes, away to Aqaba, to Amman, to Beirut, to London for some interiors, then they would go to Spain, and then to Morocco. They were, in fact, nomads, the most expensive ever, because what they were seeking was perfection. But everyone knows how careless about everything except crucial essentials true nomads are.

Silence closed behind them over the vast and empty perfection of Wadi Rumm again. Dusk faded in, deepening the blue of the sky so faintly, shade by shade, that you would have thought night would never come, and laying thin shades of gray in the air. In the limitless clarity and vastness and silence of the great valley it seemed that something overwhelming was now about to happen, the appearance of God in person, perhaps. But probably nothing will ever happen here again—it is unfitted for all things human—unless somehow or other, in some form or through some influence, Lawrence comes back.

Not far away was Petra. It is one of the sights of the world.

Petra exists in its barbaric colors and elegant architecture alone in these rock mountains of Jordan, not a ruin but an empty city, not constructed but sculptured, in rock the color of apricot, of pearl, of blue and black, and shades and swirls of all of them combined. It wasn't altered and improved and evolved in the eighteen hundred years between its great period and today. It was left. Only time acted on it, and time acted gently, because Petra was almost impregnable, even against time.

I came by car along a side road toward it and continued for a while across sparse countryside, until far ahead I began to see a vast gray rock ridge, long and knobbed and bumpy like the back of an enormous crocodile, and behind that even more formidable mountains formed into bastions and turrets and razorback ridges, which were not gray but burned purple, vaults on vaults of massive rock mountains. Petra was back in their somewhere.

The road ended. I hired a horse at the police station there in the village of Al Ji, and started down a pebbly trail through the dust, past some terraces of olive trees in the midst of the surrounding parched country. A brown horse cantered up, ridden by a black-mustached young Arab wearing a *kaffiyeh*.

"Welcome, welcome," he said. "I am Harun, official guide."

So we proceeded together down the gray-white little valley under the perfect sky, as the rock hillsides slowly closed in on both sides of us.

"Tomb," said the guide, pointing to the left. A pillared, sand-colored temple was cut into the rock there. Above the portico there were strange Egyptian-looking obelisks. It was somewhat sunken into the earth, and it also seemed to be wavering, as though I were seeing it under water, because all of its lines had been blurred by the wind and sand of two thousand years. "Come on," said the guide, as I stared at it. This wasn't anything, it seemed. Come on.

The two stone mountains now closed completely—merged in front of us—and we couldn't go on. Yes, after all, there was a cleft, a slit, wide enough so that we could ride abreast, just wide enough.

We entered this slot through the mass of rock, and coolness closed around us. The sides of this passage, which is called "the Syk," swelled and curved as we rode along, ivory white, billowy rock face. It looked as though you could reach out and mold it with your hands. It glowed with reflected sunshine coming through the opening about three hundred feet up. "For water," said Harun, pointing at a rock trough cut out of the left side of the passage. The builders of Petra didn't add to the natural rock. They went into it with their tools, and brought forth what they wanted, and in that way had made this small aqueduct.

The sides of the Syk began to turn a pale glowing orange. We wound on and on, for a mile. Finally we turned a bend, and I saw a small segment of a very beautiful classical temple filling the end of the pass.

We came out of the Syk, and just across a small open space from us, carved out of the rock cliff, was a building that the local Arabs in recent times had called the "Treasury." Its beauty made them assume that it could only contain a treasure, and since its great rooms were empty they concluded that the climax of the facade, a large urn, must conceal all the gold. They shot it more or less to pieces, but the gold never flowed. The urn was solid rock; it was a part of the cliff, like the rest of the building. Some large sculptured relief figures on it have blurred. One of the six Corinthian columns of the portico has been rebuilt.

The rest is there as it always was, sharply carved and elegant and symmetrical, unweathered because the walls of this natural courtyard had blocked the wind and sand. It consists of two classical facades, one on top of the other. The lower one might be a Greek temple, with its six columns supporting an architrave. The upper is also a classical facade, but two deep recesses break it into three vertical sections, and the central one is a small round crowned pillared pavilion, or kiosk, or lantern—a little temple within a temple.

All of it is a glowing orange, I think. The extraordinary colors of Petra are hard to label. "Rose-red city, half as old as time" is the most famous description of it. This is a very eloquent description, but not of Petra. Apricot? Smoked salmon? Unpoetic, but closer.

"Come on," said Harun. We rode on past the Treasury, which was the tomb of a king, as a matter of fact, or as much a matter of fact as anything is about Petra.

The stone cliffs fell back now as we came into the bowl among the mountains that is the center of the city. About a mile away, the other end of the bowl rose steeply to the sky.

"Theater." He pointed on the left to a curving amphitheater cut into the rock side. There was no doubt about it: it was bright purple. There were about thirty curving rows for spectators, their edges blurred, merging. Excavations were going on around the stage; a full-sized male torso in white marble lay on the ground.

All this was on the left. On the right, well up on the cliff, there was a procession—a parade—of great classical facades. "Tombs," said the guide.

I started up toward them, but my horse knew the end of the trip was near, and decided not to go there. Off he went with me, suddenly trotting briskly, toward what seemed to be—clip, clop, clip—was, in fact, a Roman street, with large smoothed paving stones now moving more quickly underhoof, stumps of pillars going rather blurringly past on the left—how did you say "Whoa!" in Arabic? Up loomed a smashed double archway, split up the central support, very shaky-looking. Clattering down the street we dived through it and then a wall, contemporary, was coming up very fast. I was still on the horse, and were we going over the wall or into it? The horse swerved toward a narrow entrance suddenly visible through the wall but couldn't make it because my weight pitched the other way and instead of bucking or jumping the horse somehow and immediately stopped. As I slid I grabbed his neck, hung, strained and pulled myself back up on the saddle where I sat still, letting my pulse get over it.

Two small Arab children ran up with bright eye, clapping. They thought I had done it on purpose. I gave each of them a shiny coin.

Petra was created by the Nabataeans, an Arabic tribe who settled there in the fourth or third century before Christ and proceeded to carve a city. It quickly became prosperous because it was astride the great east-west caravan route, and it could easily contain the biggest caravans imaginable. A handful of men could block its only entrance—the Syk—against legions. With all these potent advantages at the core, the Nabataeans spread their kingdom over the whole region and as far north as Damascus. The Greek expansion into the Near East strongly influenced them architecturally, Roman influence and power followed, and in A.D. 106 Petra passed into the Roman Empire as the capital of the province of Arabia Petraea. With the decline of Rome went the decline of Petra; such trade routes as there still were began to pass around it, and the city very gradually emptied. A large and advanced city like Petra could only live by trade and commerce. The Nabataeans thinned out, scattered, faded back into the general Arab race, leaving behind this powerful memorial of what they had been and how they had lived. For at least a thousand years it has stood empty.

That afternoon we returned on foot to the tombs my horse had avoided. There are three principal ones, side by side. The one in the middle which is often dismissed as an inferior example of the "Treasury" architecture, absorbed my attention for about an hour. It was certainly the strangest building in Petra—and perhaps anywhere. The only reason I could think of for others to pass it by was that it scared them.

It was known as the "Corinthian Tomb." Like the Treasury it had two classical facades, one on top of the other, with the lantern in the middle of the upper facade. But unlike the Treasury it was hewn out of stone that was wildly irregular in color. White, blue, red and combinations and variations of them wound in stripes across the facade, colors so vital that when it was carved it must have blazed across the city like a flag. It would still, except that rainwater pouring over it all these centuries had carried down across its face the burned red color of the cliff above, like big streaks of spilled gravy.

But it was not just that the color had run. The stone itself had run. Wind and sand and rain had pushed and blurred and corrupted the original precise stonework so that it looked like the result of some monstrous disease; the crazy lines and flowing bumps have mixed and pushed the facade all out of line, wavy and bulbous and distended it flowed on its cliff face now, all of it fantastically striped, with giant stains flowing across the stripes. It was like some gorgeous leper with its columns sinking back into the cliff and its central portal broken like a huge mouth with the teeth knocked out. The Corinthian Tomb was grand, melted, flowing and mad, like an opium dream, a rainbow Xanadu.

After this the Palace Tomb to the left of it seemed tame, even though it was three classical-facades high, the first consisting of four great portals, the second a long line of columns, and the third a ruin. The Palace Tomb had all the great size and majesty of a Roman building, but lacked the peculiar grace which the Nabataeans got into their work before the Romans came. The third tomb, the Urn Tomb, was set much further back into the cliff so that it had a column-lined forecourt, and in the interior there is an intricately ribboned orange and white colored ceiling.

There wasn't much to see inside the monuments of Petra, except solid square rooms, sometimes a niche, occasionally a stone box said to be a sarcophagus, and the tool marks on the walls, descending diagonally from right to left, very straight and very well spaced, the tool work of the Nabataeans for once seen naked.

We walked down again to the floor of the city, with the wreckage of Roman construction around us. Roman ruins can look beautiful and solid and majestic elsewhere, but here in the middle of Petra they look shoddy and negligible, not built to last.

As we started up one of the numerous narrow wadis which come steeply down the mountainsides from all directions into Petra, we heard a rather high-pitched chanting voice repeating the same words and notes over and over. It came from a cave. "Boy singing," said Harun. "Bedouin boy. That is a shop."

A shop in Petra? I looked in. The boy was making coffee over a small lamp, crouched in the dark cave. Behind him on a wooden shelf there were a few containers of simple food. Petra was in fact sometimes inhabited by a few hundred Arab nomads. They lived in the caves and raised goats.

Harun and I continued up Wadi el Farasa past many "houses"—Egyptian-looking residences of the Nabataeans, consisting of a smoothed rectangle of cliff face with a central doorway at the bottom, and at the top two horizontal carved lines running the width of the house—and past ancient temples, where the tops of the facades were decorated with a characteristic Nabataean pattern cut into the rock, two low-relief stairwaylike designs that descend from both sides and meet in the center. Further up the wadi on the right there was a classical monument—the tomb of three Roman soldiers —and opposite it a very beautiful room cut back into the rock, open, without a front. It was a banquet hall accompanying the tomb, presumably for the Nabataean version of the wake. It is an oblong, rather low-roofed room with Ionic columns in high relief along the walls. The stone of the walls was in flowing, wavering colors, a deep and rich orange shot with pearl-gray and white and thin streaks of purple, all separating and merging and interweaving so that this ancient intact banquet hall seems to move.

"Come on." On up the canyon, up the blurred remains of a large purple stairway, up a passage cut through red-and-gray-and-purple striped rock, parts of the climb steep and smooth and unprotected, not recommended for vertigo sufferers. We went on up past a dust-red elongated lion with a trough leading toward the blurred head. Did he once spout water? On we went past the remains of a Byzantine church, and at last out on a flat stone platform. This is the "High Place," and it is well named.

This was thought to have been the principal altar of the city. It must have been. We were now at the top of Petra. In the center of the platform there was a large depression cut in the rock. Next to it, on the edge of the cliff overlooking the city, was a small stone altar facing west. The Nabataeans worshiped the sun, and since this altar and a great temple high in the mountains across the valley both face west, it seems that they worshiped the setting sun. From the altar I could look across range on range of mountains, far off toward Gaza. From having been surrounded by rock mountains I felt suddenly released here: everything, all of it, was below; and beside me there was only sky, sky all around and above. Wouldn't a cave-inhabiting people put their main place of worship here, above and free of all the rock, all the weight of Petra? I could see the center of the city very, very far below: the street of columns where my horse had bolted looking tiny and frail; the great tombs and temples now were little holes and little lines. Few worshipers could have fitted up here on the platform. Did they watch an animal sacrifice from below, from in front of their rock houses, looking up across the rocks and the cliffs to this speck against the sky, and worship their god that way?

Behind me was the great gray crocodile ridge I'd first seen, and all the other outer mountains I could now see were gray too. Only this central bowl was burned purple, and only when you cut into it was the blaze of color revealed. It looked as though erosion wearing away the conventional gray surface and tops of these mountains, and the water cutting deeply into the clefts between them had finally worn away the gray stone down to the purple, and then the Nabataeans had come here and begun cutting into that. It looked as though a series of accidents had brought the gorgeous stone to daylight.

We started down from the High Place by another steep and narrow valley past stone of purest pale orange, with the usual purple powder underfoot, the stone set off by feathery little green trees and bunches of oleander in bloom here and there, down to our horses and slowly across the floor of Petra.

The unbelievable colors of the city were not what made the strongest impression; the strongest impression was made by human nobility, carved into stone. The buildings attest today to the spirit of certain people who died two thousand years ago, and that's why they are so tremendously moving—not because of their beauty but because of the heart and spirit of these extinct people emblazoned on them.

Petra is a stunning example of *hubris*—human nature defiantly surpassing all reasonable, safe limits. The creation of this city of hanging palaces, here in the middle of nowhere, was an act of blunt defiance of destiny. Petra is splendid, epic, religious, triumphant, and like all perpetrators of *hubris,* it is peculiar, isolated, and strange, living and dying in solitude.

Up another long steep narrow wadi we climbed to Ed Deir, a double temple resembling the Treasury, facing west, high on a shelf of mountain so that the setting sun, flooding across Sinai and the tomb of the biblical Aaron on a nearby spiny mountain, flamed on its facade. Out there below was the land of Moses, the wilderness where the Israelites wandered after being delivered from Egypt, the prophetic country of the Old Testament, the land of God-haunted, suffering, warring tribes, the deserts of holy men and the cities to be sacked, and Sodom and Gomorrah, and the Dead Sea and the Red Sea and sackcloth and ashes, all the bedraggled, scarecrow turmoil of the Testaments; and in their midst, superb Petra, its glorious temples lifted above all of that and level only with the sun, miraculous Petra alone in its achievement, impregnable, magnificent—too magnificent not only to last itself but to contribute to life anything lasting. What the humbler biblical peoples all around them did and thought is still alive in our civilization today, but the Nabataeans, flying up there so close to the sun, fell from such a height they dropped out of life forever.

We descended to the center of the city again, and I had a simple supper in a little brick rest house there. Coming out afterward, I found the vast dark recesses springing silently to life: Bedouin families had moved for a time into orange caves and temples all around; and their evening fires were going, creating bright orange half-moons flickering on all sides of the great dark city, silent glowing grottoes of orange fire hanging everywhere, while a star-crowded Arab sky closed like a lid overhead.

As I was taking all this in, like an immense practical joke the Grieg "Piano Concerto" began to sweep out of one of the caves and cross the city, its ripe excitable passages inundating the stone valleys, all the splashy nervousness and emotionalism of the music flooding through the impassive city.

I followed the tumult, and it led to a small cave not far away where a man was lying on a sleeping bag, apparently drinking in the music and contemplating the stars. As the chords crashed back and forth across the city he came to himself, sat up, and I recognized him as a young British doctor I had met in Amman, sent into the desert by a charitable organization to treat the Bedouin. He carried a battery phonograph and a few records everywhere he went. We talked for a while as Grieg passionately washed over the silent Bedouin at their fires, and finally the doctor stopped playing the music, and one by one the orange grottoes went black.

Then finally I began to make my way to Jerusalem on a horse, out across Petra, through the Syk, to the rendezvous at a well with the hired car and driver, along the road through Ma'an to Amman again, taking there the road west down into the dead whiteness of the Dead Sea Valley, across that pan of heat, through the police checkpoint at the River Jordan, seeing there the bend in the little stream where Christ was baptized, to Jericho and the excavation of its ancient wall, past another mud and tin hodgepodge shantytown —"home" for some of the half-million refugees who fled into Jordan during the Palestine War of 1948–1949 and have festered there ever since—past the Dead Sea Scroll caves and Mount Nebo where Moses saw the Promised Land, and so into it.

After a long climb up from the vast depression of the Dead Sea, up steadily through the hills of Judaea, arriving finally at the top of the mountain ridge which runs north and south through Palestine, the car came in sight of the lofty crest, from where the country drops down again to the Mediterranean shore; Bethany was off to the right and Bethlehem was on the left, and in front, crowning the hills, were some very long, dark gold battlements, with a lighter gold dome hovering behind them, and several slim towers also rising above the crenellated wall: Jerusalem.

Cypresses and palms and olive trees were spread over the hillside below the battlements, and certain churches and towers could be seen amid the hills outside the wall.

We drove on to one of the great gates, and from there a porter helped me carry my bags to a hostel operated by the Dominican monks inside the Old City. Walking along the narrow hall-like market ways under an arching roof broken by openings now and then so that the passage was striped with sunshine, with countrywomen in long and beautiful dressses and white veils going by me on donkeys, I began to feel suddenly and inexplicably happy. It was something the city itself gave me. Once before a city had done this, Venice; in spite of everything, Venice. Now here it was again, stones transmitting happiness. How or why it happened was unanswerable; I just felt that I could spend the rest of my life in Jerusalem.

It had to do with the stone, first of all. Everywhere in Jordan there had been stone, from the million dead pebbles of the desert, to the pink and white rock being diligently chipped to fit the Amman amphitheater, to the great achievements cut forth from the cliffs of Petra, and here underfoot were great worn stone blocks of Jerusalem's passages—yellow, ivory, tan, gold, gray—bordered by stone walls of numberless cloisters and churches and academies and museums and mosques and shrines. Coming from a wood country, I was exhilarated by these streets and walls and palaces and gates so well made with so much fine stone.

And it had to do with the air, clean as outer space, moving through these tragic streets, making even the marked Stations of the Cross ("Christ Falls a Third Time") a little less grim, and softening even the look of the latest of the city's many disasters, the frozen battlefield of no-man's-land running its fantastic course through the heart of the Holy City. And then there were the bells, clear and musical, that sounded along the rooftops; and there was also a kind of purposeful, measured pace to the life of Jerusalem.

And it had to do with the people, like Miss Douglas-Scotti, of Italy. We had our spaghetti and red wine next to each other in the hostel refectory every day; Miss Douglas-Scotti had spent a large part of these middle years of hers going on devotional trips to Christian shrines up and down the Mediterranean. She had an unusually fair, scrubbed, northern face for an Italian woman, and as her name suggested she was Scottish by descent, eight hundred years removed from Scotland. In the evenings she and I sometimes took an Italian-style evening stroll through the arcades and passages of Jerusalem, while she cheerfully described to me her many pilgrimages, voyages which seemed to combine both reverence and distraction, as though for her finding God was a lifetime treasure hunt, with clues leading from Lourdes to Rocamadour to Rome to Jerusalem.

And it had to do with the sobriety of the city. There were no bars, nightclubs, theaters, or anything similar within the walls. No one has ever described me as an ascetic, but it was a relief to be free of all that for once: no bright lights blazing, no music jarring, no posters blaring, no marquees and no barkers and no neon and no jukeboxes and no blue jeans and no toreador pants, no one whose business it was to tempt, except the devil. It was like being a schoolboy again, getting up and going to bed at naive hours, with constructive things to do between.

The Jordanian administration operated Jerusalem with complete fairness and impartiality to the Christian communities, if with a certain ironical amusement. The scramble of the Christian sects for possession of the Holy Places probably is, from the Moslem point of view, pretty funny to watch. The Greek Orthodox Church has, so to speak, the ground floor, with the Roman Catholic Church in firm possession of the mezzanine. The Armenian, Assyrian, Coptic, and Ethiopian churches all have squatters' rights, while the Protestant Church is completely excluded, having to content itself with building churches where nothing happened, and discovering a "Christ's Tomb" which, just because it looks the way Christ's tomb looked at the time, surely isn't it, and the unrecognizable marble cell, strung with holy lamps in the Church of the Holy Sepulcher, probably is. The art and architecture and atmosphere of the Holy Places is Byzantine, two-dimensional, marble and gilt, dark and cavelike, full of flickering lamps and ancient incense. I didn't like it at all at first, all the flat gloomy opulence of it. And then thinking about America, where so many churches seem to have much more the feeling of the Houses of Congress than of any spiritual place, I felt that it was my past, and not Jerusalem's, that was at fault. This was Christianity here, and it always had been. America was a place where religion had been too often turned into a kind of extension of the Community Chest, a worthy cause, not entirely unlike Little League baseball. In these murky caves of Palestine its roots in mystery and miracles and suffering were darkly invoked.

A tourist policeman had been assigned to take me around Jerusalem, a jolly plump Moslem in green uniform and piked helmet, and he watched with sardonic, Islamic glee my reaction inside that vast, black Byzantine fortress, the Church of the Holy Sepulcher, as he led me up some stairs to a darkly gleaming chapel, a chapel marking the spot of Mount Calvary. I had been brought up in all the traditions of conservative Christianity, and finding myself suddenly on Calvary stripped me to a total and unprepared-for awe; I thought I might fall on my face, and as the policeman led me up to the three altars—Greek, Roman, and Armenian Catholic—which elbow each other for the privilege of marking this spot, a little Orthodox monk emerged from the shadows, and amid the flashing of candles on silver and the air of incense, he mechanically said something in English. "Forty cents," I understood him to say, and as I stared at him incredulously the policeman easily and with a faint smile reached into his pocket and handed him a coin. Then he led me out of the chapel.

We went also to Bethlehem, to the gleaming marble crypt under the Church of the Nativity, where Christ was born. Touched, visited, prayed in all these centuries, it naturally bears no resemblance to what it was originally. And looking at it was like contemplating one atomic bomb: the potentialities were so infinitely greater than what was visible that no real connection could be made.

Then, squaring his shoulders, my guide took me back to Jerusalem, where the most important site happens to be occupied by the Moslem religion. This news is not widely circulated in the West. Here were the dome and tower I had seen from outside the battlements, the dome covering an exposed rock where Mohammed stopped on his way to heaven, and also where Abraham had prepared to sacrifice his son Isaac. The Dome of the Rock is a small, octagonal structure of extreme beauty, tiled on the outside, covered with richly beautiful mosaics within; they do not portray anything but simply form patterns, in the Moslem custom.

The towers belong to El-Aksa Mosque, an enormous, high-rectangular marble hall, thickly and richly rugged, hung with vast chandeliers, and otherwise empty, like all mosques. The simplicity of the Moslem religion was something I had not been prepared for; set beside the Byzantine extravagance of the Christian shrines, it made a striking contrast. The human form is never portrayed, lest some vestige of idolatory cling to it. Also, no one asked me for forty cents: a fee for a guide book was charged at the entry to the precincts, and there was no more money-changing anywhere.

The Holy Places were not what signified most to me in Jerusalem in any case but rather Jerusalem itself, the shepherds in the hills, the donkeys and the women in veils, the stones and the air, the tiny shops of the bazaars, Miss Douglas-Scotti with her itinerant devoutness, a young Orthodox monk gazing in delight over his shoulder at his cape fanning out behind him, flamelike cypresses in the cobbled courtyard of the Nobel Sanctuary, the sense of many scholars and young theological students and old sages cloistered in towers, all occupied in this ancient highland city with preserving the past but busy in the present as well, rendering unto Caesar (King Hussein, that would be) the things that were his, and unto Christ and Mohammed and Abraham the things that were theirs.

One afternoon outside the walls I walked up to an impressive onion-domed church that faced the city from a steep hillside of trees. A few nuns were attached to it still, although like the other great Russian establishments in Jerusalem it had been withering since the great patronage of the Czars ended.

In a crypt off the refectory in the cellar is the tomb of a lady. She is buried here because Jerusalem is Jerusalem, where three great religions—in spite of everything, including themselves, are focused on God, here where the pilgrimages end.

Hers began in Hesse-Darmstadt, in Germany, where she was born a princess, a granddaughter of Queen Victoria, in 1864. She and her sisters became the quintessence of Victorianism, since their mother died early and they were in great part raised by Queen Victoria herself. Probably from her they acquired the lofty idealism, the dedication to duty, the sense of high mission which makes the Victorian period seem so admirable and unreasonable to people today. One of her sisters married the Marquess of Milford Haven, and another married the Czar of Russia.

In 1884, she herself married the Russian Grand Duke Sergei Alexandrovich. As the Grand Duchess Elizabeth Feodorovna, she lived in the greatest luxury in Moscow, where the Grand Duke was an extremely reactionary Governor General. The Grand Duchess was beautiful, her jewels and clothes and palaces and way of life were magnificent, but despite this hothouse life of privilege, she did not lose sight of the high goals she thought life should be focused on. As most kind, good, idealistic people seem to do, she had married a monster. The Grand Duke was insanely jealous, humiliated her in public, censored her mail, regulated her reading, oppressed her spirit. She never complained, never considered any escape; she had taken the marriage vows, and would unquestioningly fulfill them until death, of course.

One day in 1905, coming out of her palace, she heard a loud explosion, seemed to know what it meant, rushed to Kremlin Square, and with her own hands picked up the pieces of the Grand Duke Sergei.

The young anarchist who had thrown the bomb was caught, and she visited him in his cell before his execution to plead for his soul, for his salvation, for his repentance before God. She made no impression; they might as well have been speaking different languages. She urged him to read a Bible she had brought. That made no impression either; he told her he had something he himself had written for her to read instead: the bitter story of his own bitter life.

The assassination and the assassin released all the idealism and spirituality in her completely. She disposed of her great collection of jewelry including her wedding ring, and after that wore only a wooden cross. She no longer ate anything that had once been alive, subsisting on milk, vegetables, and bread. She slept on a board, and organized an order of nuns to work among the neediest people in Russia. As a nun, she redoubled her work and prayers when the First World War broke out. While leading this dedicated life she did not lose contact with the world, both through her good deeds on the lowest level and her influence on the highest; she understood the destructive influence of Rasputin on her sister the Empress Alexandra and on Russia, and struggled to end it. Like everyone else, she failed to penetrate Alexandra's deluded dream that Rasputin was the instrument of God. The Russian Revolution broke out in 1917, and for a while this blameless, self-sacrificing woman dedicated to good works was left alone by the revolutionaries. But in 1918 the Bolsheviks, fighting in the name of the same poor and afflicted she had devoted herself to, arrested her, shipped her to Siberia, and in July, 1918, on the night after her sister had been slaughtered in a cellar not too far away, she was thrown down a mine shaft with some other relatives, and bombs were thrown down after them. The anti-Bolshevik army retook the area soon after, and from the evidence found in the mine concluded that the Grand Duchess Elizabeth Feodorovna had lived for some time after the fall and the explosions.

Her remains were shipped out of Russia by way of China, and through the efforts of her surviving sister in England, they were sent by ship to Port Said in Egypt, and then buried here, in Jerusalem. It seemed the only place for her.

There used to be a certain kind of gallantry in the world: once people tried to be noble and didn't seem peculiar doing it: there used to be something called idealism, and it was taken seriously. Elizabeth Feodorovna was a sterling symbol of all that shining nineteenth century spirit, and the anarchist who blew up the Grand Duke and thrust his own bitter life story at her in justification was the twentieth century spirit being born. Instead of duty, the twentieth century believed in self-realization; in place of ideals, instincts; in place of an ultimate sense of mission, an ultimate meaninglessness.

The jovial Moslem policeman took me to see the Mandelbaum Gate, the only connection between the part of Palestine now in Jordan and the part in Israel. It exists for United Nations personnel to pass back and forth in their duties of policing the Armistice line, and for travelers, who, with proper documents, may cross from one belligerent to the other, on foot only.

We drove past some antitank emplacements and up to a wooden bar. Two Jordanian soldiers and a civilian were playing cards beside it. Beyond it was no-man's-land, and on the other side of that, a few dozen yards away, was Israel. No-man's-land ran straight through Jerusalem, and represented the battle lines as they were when the Armistice was declared in 1949. There was still only an Armistice all these years later, and that was what made this frozen, aging battlefield so uncanny. The policeman and I walked past the barrier, perhaps ten yards into no-man's-land. Parts of buildings sagged behind tangles of barbed wire. Semi-intact buildings had windows full of sandbags along the rim of this chaos, presumably with soldiers behind them. Up and down this strip of land could be seen the full shambles of war, all there in its motionless violence, splitting Jerusalem in two. I didn't know of any comparable situation to this anywhere in history; it seemed to exist only in art, in comedy. It reminded me of an old Laurel and Hardy movie, as a matter of fact: vacant-faced Laurel dutifully patrolling up and down in some isolated pocket of the Western Front ten years after the First World War had ended.

I stared across at Israel, where because of a typically Near-Eastern muddle, I wasn't able to go. I had felt its influence all over Jordan, and wanted very much to see for myself. I often thought in Jordan that the creation of Israel was the best thing that had happened to the Arab countries in a long time, since it supplied the necessary goad and affront to their pride needed to force them into the twentieth century, but I didn't expect them to see it that way.

Standing here in this uncontrolled strip of land between the two, it seemed to me that I had found the place and point of view from where all the Near East could be seen—the Near East where Saudi Arabia has been having its palace risings, Jordan its repeated insurrections, where Iraq has gone through two bloody revolutions and Syria has had one coup after another, where Lebanon has had a civil war, Egypt a profound revolution, and Yemen a revolution followed by a civil war, all of them meanwhile permanently hostile to Israel. This was the Near East: a paralyzed battlefield.

Part

THE AEGEAN

HYDRA AMORGOS DELOS ATHOS

MYKONOS SIFNOS KALYMNOS

Four

In one way, I was glad not to be able to go to Israel, because I had been away from America for many months, and I was daily getting more interested in it again, beginning to feel almost like an Arab or a European who had never been there. The numb unresponsiveness which had invaded me there had reached bottom at the tepid pool and in the arid nightclub and on the torpid porch of the Hotel Philadelphia in Amman, and I was now rapidly coming around. Was America as flat, stale and bleak as I remembered? I saw things differently now.

The winter months had passed, and then, as I was about ready to return to America, I received an invitation to join a group of friends yachting in the Greek islands. It wasn't every day that I got such an invitation, and remembering Forster's unemphatic recommendation and his murmured "it's the people," I immediately decided to go.

Space, silence and emptiness were the elements of this Aegean world as we sailed into it. Space, silence and emptiness; it was as though some loudspeaker bawling in our ears for so long we were no longer conscious of it had suddenly ceased, and we were relieved more than had seemed possible.

Ahead of us in the sea that first day in June appeared a boat, one. It came wallowing out of the blue haze toward us, a caïque, with high bow and stern, wide amidships, the mainsail at an angle, the hull painted a fresh and pretty blue striped with green. It was clearly going out of its way to pass close to us, and our pilot shifted course, too, to pass close to it. There was no reason for any recognition or exchange between the two ships, but it was *lonely* out here, each wanted a good look at the other, to see new human faces, if for no other reason. The caïque, pitching a little, passed by quite near us; in the little cabin door the skipper eyed us intently, and the cabin boy practically danced on deck as he waved. We waved and shouted back, and then went on into the bluish solitude, toward the island of Hydra in the haze ahead.

Hydra came out of the haze and into knockout clarity very fast.

We sailed along its forbidding cliff shoreline until we came to a natural bowl in the rock face, an amphitheater curving back from the sea, with white houses climbing gradually and then steeply up toward the surrounding rock cliffs. It looked like the setting for some ideal musical comedy, and as we sailed into this little port at noon past an old cannon emplacement on the left and a seawall on the right, a bell began to toll melodiously, as though on cue in the theater. It came from a stone bell tower in the center of the port. From the portal at the foot of the tower a procession slowly moved out into the sparkling sunlight. Leading it was an acolyte holding a palm design on a long pole, and after him came others holding medallions on long poles, then priests in white cassocks and black hats, and finally several men carrying a handsome and strangely happy-looking coffin.

Following that came a small crowd, including naval officers in white. This pageant moved along the colorful quay, turned into a little street between two lively cafés, and wound slowly up toward a piece of ground on a promontory above the port that was full of those prizes in Greece, trees, including a number of splendid cypresses, and of white mausoleums.

As a funeral, it was a failure. The bell could only toll musically, the water danced in the snappy breeze, the white houses sparkled, the blue sky glowed, and the white cassocks flashed in the sunshine. Death itself looked happy on the Greek islands.

By two o'clock in the afternon the wharf, or the "Agora" (market) was deserted. Sailors slept in the shade of their caïques, a waiter in one of the small restaurants carefully put two tables together in the shade, laid himself out like a corpse on top of them, his hands folded on his chest, and fell asleep.

For some reason or other I set off across the empty shadeless cobblestones of the Agora, becoming the only thing moving there. The sunshine immediately came down so heavily on my head and shoulders that I was forced into a reverie, feeling forgetful and reflective but with nothing to forget and nothing to reflect on, the inside of my head becoming like a movie house that had been flooded with sunshine and so put out of operation, no images visible because everywhere there was light; I ambled on over the cobbles, wondering hazily how far it was to the shade of a wall at the other end of Agora, feeling content, slowly asking myself whether the sun hadn't drifted a little closer than ever before to the earth today and whether in a minute I might smell my hair beginning to smolder, because on this particular afternoon the sun had come just a little too close for the first time in history. That's the kind of sun it was. Eventually I made it to the strip of shade, and began to realize that the people of these islands spend three or four months every year under that implacable sun and the influence it must have on their lives.

Twelve weeks later, when I was again on Hydra, I saw a cloud, my first Greek cloud. It gathered its small white self together in the pure blueness of the sky, and in a lonely way sailed across the sky and off in the direction of Russia. Everybody stopped whatever they were doing to look wonderingly at it.

The sun was always there, all summer long, and nothing ever stood between it and the Aegean islands except a thin haze occasionally. The sun burned down strongly at seven in the morning, and was still pouring down at seven at night.

We had lunch at a café on the Agora, at a plain wooden table on the marble-like paving stones. There was nothing fussy about the restaurant or about the food; there was nothing fussy, I learned as the summer wore on, about Greece.

A gust of wind suddenly plunged across the Agora at us, driving the big canvas awning over the café wildly back and forth on its guide wires, and then drifting away again and leaving calmness behind. We went on eating. Abruptly another gust hurled itself on us; this time a waiter was standing next to the awning, and he grabbed it. A moment later he found himself ten feet in the air, and he swung there for a few moments while the Greeks roared with laughter, and then he fell swinging back to earth, breathing heavily but with a game grin. Calmness again ensued, and then after a few more minutes the wind once again hurled itself on us.

The Aegean wind, turbulent as madness, was one of the fundamental facts of life on these islands. Work, going to sea, sleep, tempers, all were deeply conditioned by it; it was as strong a force there as the sun itself.

After lunch I went to a pile of boulders going down to the sea near the port for a swim. Raw gusts of wind had whipped the sea into engulfing the lower rocks, where there were ladders for people to get in and out of the water. Today they would have to sweep up to a ladder on the crest of a wave, catch it and pull themselves up before the heavy receding wave dragged them across the rocks beneath the ladder. Most of the two-dozen people there were therefore not going in; in fact, when I arrived there was only one bather, a large woman bobbing placidly enough from crest to foaming crest.

Eventually she decided to come out. I watched, we all watched her bob along toward the rocks and the ladder. She maneuvered herself within about ten feet of them, and then started forward with a wave. But in her slowness she lost the wave which swept up to the ladder ahead of her and then quickly receded, leaving a gulf which revealed the jagged rocks below, toward which she began to be rushed by the next rapidly approaching wave. Desperately flailing backward, the woman managed to beat away from being dashed by its full impact against the rocks; she disappeared in a swirl of foam and then came bobbing and panting to the windswept surface again.

There were six young Greek men on the rocks; they reacted as though they were one. Into the sea they catapulted in good and bad dives, and quickly all of them were around the distressed swimmer, supporting her and pulling and tugging and working her toward the rocks again. A wave rose up behind them all, and the group splashed and bobbed up to the rocks and ladder. Two of the Greeks were flung against the rocks, but the woman in the middle was shielded by them, and two others fixed her hands at the right instant onto a rung of the ladder, and as they were scraped back across the rocks by the receding waves she managed to pull herself to safety. Then the young men, three of them bleeding from bruises, came out of the water themselves.

It was a brave exhibition, and when one of the rescuers sat down near me to dab his scraped leg with a towel I congratulated him. "Thank you," he said, smiling happily, "it was nothing." Reflecting on the nobility and stoicism of classical Greece, I thought this was a surviving streak of it. "Here four thousand of the Peloponnese once fought with three thousand thousand. . . . Stranger, go tell the Spartans that we lie here obedient to their word," reads the famous memorial to the heroic dead at Thermopylae. That was the spirit.

We gathered again at dusk aboard the *Toscana.* Around us the natural amphitheater of Hydra rose on three sides. All the life of the island was concentrated here; a dusty track or two trailed away from it for short distances along the sides of the cliff and then petered out. There were no vehicles of any kind on the island; donkeys were the only transportation. There was one telephone, at the post office. There was of course no television, as there was not anywhere in Greece. There was "running water" in some houses, in a manner of speaking. It ran this way. A boat would arrive in the port at unstated intervals pulling behind it what seemed an enormous black sea monster, or the world's biggest sausage; this apparition contained fresh water. When it appeared men began hurriedly stringing fire hoses up the steep narrow streets and stairways of Hydra, harried by householders who might have been without water for a few days or a few weeks. Like a great serpent, the hose uncoiled itself up the winding ways, came in through the door, and thrusting its head into the cistern, began to spew water. When it receded again the householder could pump by hand, or if his house was very up-to-date, by motor, the water from his cistern to the tank at the top of the house, and from there it ran through whatever plumbing there was. Drinking water, on the other hand, came from a spring on the island by donkey, and was stored in a large biblical pot in the kitchen. Ice came from the icehouse. Fish and fruit was bought from boats which came to the harbor. Medical attention came from the mayor or from midwives.

We sat at dusk aboard the *Toscana* contemplating this beautiful fishing village and barnyard, Hydra, with its flimsy waterfront fringe of Athenian teen-age night life.

A successful Athenian businessman and his wife, who had a summer house on Hydra, came on board for dinner. They were both middle-aged, medium-sized, elegantly dressed, and fluent in English. They were friends of friends, and so we introduced ourselves: Henry McIlhenny, who had chartered the *Toscana* and invited the rest of us on the cruise, a curator at the Philadelphia Museum, possessor of a great art collection himself including some of the pillars of French Impressionism; Joseph Pulitzer, Jr., editor and publisher of the St. Louis *Post-Dispatch,* and his wife Louise; the Philadelphia artist and teacher Emlen Etting and his wife Gloria Braggiotti Etting, who was in the midst of her second book and compiling a lecture based on this trip; the young New York composer Charles Turner; Perry Rathbone, director of the Boston Museum of Fine Arts; Mrs. Patricia Clark of Philadelphia, charming widow; and myself, itinerant author.

We asked them about the people of Hydra. "Back behind the port live the real Hydriots, who find what work there is fishing and in construction and so on. There's not much work for them here. They're very self-respecting, they have their pride, and of course they look down on us Athenians as being weak and corrupted, city people. They have the strong characters of islanders."

"Some of them are superstitious," his wife put in. "Several of the less educated type of men here, after they speak to me, spit! Just like that, matter-of-factly. To ward off the Evil Eye. I've gotten more or less used to it. A woman who works for us here has never been down to the port. She's in her fifties. It wasn't respectable to come here when she was a girl. I'm not sure she's ever seen the sea at close range."

"They get enough money to live," he went on, "from relatives abroad, as so many Greeks do. You know our families are very tightly knit, and it is the duty of those making money to support the others. Most of the families here have sons or brothers in the Greek Merchant Marine, and they send part of their pay back, out of the little they earn. There are only about twenty-five hundred people living here permanently, but this rock won't support even that many."

"To be a Greek man," she said with a twinkle in her eye, "is a very, as you say, mixed blessing. Dimitris will agree with me here. From the moment they are born they are cherished by their mothers and sisters, they are superior to women, they are served; after they are married they are still free to come and go; they are free, free. Paradise! But how they pay for it! A young Greek man may not marry until his sisters have their dowries and are married. No wonder they serve him! If a Greek man has an ugly sister and doesn't make much money—bachelorhood for life. There are a number here on Hydra."

"The worst time for these people," said Dimitris, "was during the German occupation in the war. They simply starved. Practically nothing can be grown here, the only food was on the Peloponnesus," he waved at it rising in range on range of beautiful hills four miles away across the water, "and it was very expensive. The Hydriots had to sell everything to stay alive. Some of them tore down their houses and sold the materials to get food.

"Very grim story. Excuse me. On the other hand," leaning back and making an open-handed gesture, "these people here, and for that matter all Greeks, have a capacity to enjoy themselves. It's true. That's one thing we really know how to do. We can do it with almost nothing at all if necessary. Have you ever noticed a Greek taking pleasure in a flower, or a cup of coffee? We are able to create a gay party for twelve people with two pistachio nuts, half a glass of wine and a harmonica! We can respond to any encouragement for enjoying life faster than anybody, and go further with it. We laugh, and we make jokes, and we sing a lot, we sing to ourselves or together or anywhere, and we like to dance very much. We believe, we know, that life is to be enjoyed, and since most people here are poorer than anyone else in Europe or America, you can see how strong this force must be in the Greeks, in spite of so much misery, economic misery. We feel it in our bones, life is to be enjoyed. There's an engine always running inside a Greek, something like a generator building up the potential for joy. When you switch into that, out it pours!

"Take my son for example. He's a student here at the Merchant Navy School," and he indicated a large plain stone building overlooking the harbor. "He and three of his classmates were at a little house my brother has on the mainland one weekend. It's an extremely simple little farm place, just used for weekends, no electricity, no radio, no neighbors. How were these four active young men going to enjoy themselves? One of them began absentmindedly tapping a glass with a spoon. Then another tapped a half-full bottle with a fork. My son picked up the top of a pot that had a loose handle. He shook it. It rattled. The fourth one began establishing a sort of underlying rhythm by tapping on the table, and very soon they were doing all kinds of rhythms and variations, some of them pretty complicated, some of them very funny. Then, keeping the rhythm, they sang one of our Greek songs, dividing into parts. They did a Greek men's dance, supplying their own music. It's a rather complicated dance, and they added some complications of their own. By now they'd completely forgotten what a bleak place they were staying in. What else did they do? They did a burlesque of the drill they do at the school. Uproarious. Then they combined all the rhythm and the music they were making into the most elaborate version you can imagine of your march, "Stars and Stripes Forever!" It was a wonderful evening for everybody. And with no artificial stimulation at all, not even a guitar. No. From someone tapping a glass with a fork. Those are the Greeks."

"It helps to be a little crazy," his wife put in. "All Greeks are that too. There's something called the 'Greek madness.' We don't have all those complexes you go to psychiatrists for in America. No. Nothing as ambiguous as all those American complexes. But a Greek has one devastating obsession inside him. Scratch a Greek and you will find an obsession."

"I think we haven't completely forgotten our old gods," said Dimitris. "We all still think that if we achieve some wonderful thing, why, we'll go straight to Olympus, to immortality! Either that, or else we sometimes suddenly throw our lives away."

"Like poor Costas," said his wife.

"Like poor Costas, a friend of ours in the shipping business. He's young, successful, handsome and, as he has to be in that business, very tough. He was in his thirties before he had time to get married, and then before the wedding the girl changed her mind, married another man. I thought Costas might kill the other one, or perhaps the girl. It would have been characteristic of the way he behaved. But what did he do? He went to bed for two months, and cried. Cried! There's no way of knowing about Greeks."

"Or poor Tassos," said his wife.

"That one," chuckled Dimitris. "He's a school friend of our son's. He's usually at the head of the class, the responsible type people give authority to, sensible and calm and firm. All the other boys tended to defer to his judgment on things at the school. Well, last summer he had nothing to do, and so he started drinking *ouzo!* It's of course very strong, but he didn't notice how much he was drinking, and he began drinking one bottle a day and then two bottles a day and reading or listening to the radio and drinking and drinking and drinking, but the point was he *didn't really notice what he was doing.* He couldn't understand why after a while he couldn't see straight! At last he got so sick that he went to a doctor, to find out what could be the matter with him! Never mentioned the *ouzo,* of course. The doctor found it out at last in the examination, and he said that the boy was not very far from killing himself *without noticing it.* It was this strange thing in the Greek character. It is as though we can be taken over by a stranger."

Around us, in the great natural amphitheater crowded with white houses, the night sounds of Hydra were asserting themselves, the crazy roosters breaking out at any and all times, crowing back and forth across the silent rooftops; donkeys braying agonizingly; and now and then a shriek from the cats.

The Hydra tribe of cats gave the impression that if the human population diminished just a little more, they, the cats, would take over the island. Their scarred, emaciated bodies moved not only stealthily but rapaciously among the tables of the Agora, and slunk along the steps and alleys, pilfering. Often they had an eye gone, and the remaining one glowed with deepened evil. As I learned later when living on Hydra, one of them in the black of night might drop like an infiltrator onto the windowsill, and calmly explore around you as you slept. If you woke up and hissed or yelled at it, the cat would glower steadily back at you for a while and then coldly withdraw, for a while. Or, in returning to your house you opened the front door, and there was a sudden scrape of claws and a ragged shape, or two, or three, or four, shot by you and out the door. You felt relieved, because they had bolted for the door and not for you.

The few dogs on Hydra saved scraps of their self-respect by pretending that there were no cats on the island. "That's not a cat," they seemed to say to themselves as they trotted briskly past some battler, "it may look like a cat, but I know it's not." Occasionally a new dog would arrive on Hydra and make the natural, elsewhere, move of chasing a cat, only to find to his dumbfounderment that the cats here, far from running away, turned on him regardless of his size with the fury of burning witches, quickly supported by other shrieking harpies, and one more Hydra dog was created.

After dinner on the *Toscana* we started in a group along one side of the port to a foot road cut into the rocky hillside above the sea; turning into this little road we encountered the moon, clarion-clear in the ash-black sky, spreading a wide field of silver on the black water. Big and little stars were scattered everywhere around it, and the lights of other islands on the horizon could be seen past the great shadowy palisades that lined the coast of Hydra like the bastions of a vast fortress. A tiny motor launch with a fringed cloth roof puttered slowly across this wide silver sea; on board some people were singing, one of the convoluted, dirgelike songs of Greece.

We came to a kind of nightclub in a one-story stone building where small boats had been built until recently. There was one still there, suspended from the ceiling, and another served as a bar. In the dimly lit room the young set, mostly Greek, danced to popular European songs and American rock-'n-roll and Greek music.

At the bar I suddenly found myself next to the young

Greek who had taken part in the rescue that afternoon. He was drunk.

"I am drunk," he said. "Somebody gave me whisky, and so," a wide and happy grin, "I am drunk."

I said that he had a right to celebrate after the rescue that afternoon.

"You know something? I have to tell you something." His eyes narrowed, the direct manner now became point-blank. "I didn't do it for her. I did it for myself. For the glory. I and all the others went in to save her because we saw a chance for a little bit of glory. I was furious because the others went in, and they were all furious too. We all wanted to be noticed, we all wanted a chance to—distinguish ourselves. What do you expect? How are we going to do anything in Greece, make any kind of mark, be *remembered?* How? Be successful in business or some other kind of a career? There's hardly any success for anybody in Greece. I will earn four thousand drachmas—$133—a month, and so will my friends. I will live with my wife in a house like theirs, our clothes will be the same, I will have the same everything that they will have and nothing more. I can't show what *I* am myself, there is no way to show that, except by some extraordinary act. I would gladly die in a war if I could be a hero, I don't care about dying, because then I would have done something and distinguished myself and be remembered. Well," he shrugged, "I did my best today. I pulled one-sixth of a fat lady out of the water. I guess I'm not immortal yet after that, though, am I?"

Out the window went my concept that the nobility of classical Greece survived there today, and then it came back in again. What else had inspired the ancient heroes, and even more, the ancient rank and file, at least after heroically repelling the Persians, except glory, unless it was the even less noble goals of money and booty? "Stranger, go tell the

Spartans that we lie here obedient to their word." Don't let them forget us and what we have done. Remind them about us. Us.

The young Greek beside me, noticing through his haze that I wasn't shocked by this confession, forged ahead, determined that I should think badly of him and of other Greeks. They want to be thought of as devils, clever devils. "We are malicious, we Greeks. I will go to the greatest trouble to trick *one* drachma away from you. Why? For one drachma? Of course not. To prove I am cleverer than you. To make myself feel better."

I thought after much more experience in Greece that there was a certain amount of truth in this. But on the other hand, a Greek's attention span is often short, and may be interrupted at a key turning in the deception, so that as likely as not he will subtract from your bill instead of adding to it.

Our party stepped back into the daunting glory of the night, and walked along the pebbled way, beside the stone wall, on the rocky cliff. The moon was shattering on the sea. There was guitar music coming from somewhere. We passed a poor, stark little restaurant, vast wine barrels at the rear of it, crude wooden tables on the concrete floor. The food was sure to be no good; the food was rarely good in Greece, nature not supplying good ingredients and cooks not being very resourceful. There were a few delicious specialties; the rest was just food.

Everything was sparse on Hydra and on the Greek islands generally. Many of the people carried a flower, one; it reassured them to have one flower. Ofter they gave it to you as a token of friendliness. In the main square on many islands there was one tree, a vast spreading survivor with limbs supported by sticks like a very old man, one huge and beautiful old tree; the people had been forced to cut down all the others by some crisis or emergency, and this one alone remained, spared as a memorial, a token, and almost an object of worship—nowhere do trees look as sacred as in parched Greece; a fisherman returned in his little boat with *one* good big fish; on the terrace of a house there was only one plant, but it was a beautiful one; on the highest peak of the islands there was one structure, always a tiny white chapel unless it was a monastery; there was one well, one grove of trees, one sea gull, one party, one dress, one drink.

The following evening we tied up in the great natural harbor of Poros, the town a tumble of white above us, the Peloponnesus now a magnificent cypress-strewn plain just across a channel of the sea, so close that Poros seemed hardly an island at all. Down to us along the water came plinking, wailing, half-oriental music, and we followed it to a little *taverna* on the waterfront. A man was playing a *bouzoukia*—a Greek variation of the mandolin, another fiddled, and the third played a Greek bagpipe made from the skin of a goat.

You either like Greek music or you don't. Wailing, rhythmic, compelling, it is in the minor mode associated in the West with sadness but here with sensuality; either it intrigues you, or it gets on your nerves.

But even the people of the Aegean who didn't like it weren't irritated by it. I didn't see any irritated people during my months there; the islanders did not seem to irritate. Very occasionally they exploded with anger, but that characteristic minor fever of our world, irritation, was outside their range, burned out by the sun and blown away by the *meltemi*. Their responses were all more fundamental than that; little things didn't bother them, and to big things they responded directly; irritation, letting your emotions skid uncertainly along the edge of some unpleasantness, wasn't in them.

You either like Greek music or you don't; you either like Greece or you don't. It is not a lovable country in the way that Italy is, not all flowers and smiles and music and warmth. It is angular, intent, selected and either very sober or very gay. Much of the land is uncompromisingly stark, in keeping with the ruthless power of the summer sun and the obstreperousness of the winds. It is also an extremely dramatic land to look at. The sweep of the plain opposite us now on the Peloponnesus was one example, as was the great plain of Attica rolling up to Athens and on to the mountains behind, and the extraordinary mountains of Arcadia, and the fantastic mount of Mycenae with the corridor of land before it rolling down to the sea, and the Acropolis itself of course, and thousands of less famous or entirely anonymous panoramas and corners which were innately dramatic: a little mill, for example, with a chapel leading into a cave behind it, a millpond in front with a few ducks on it, one vast tree beside it, and a rock mountain rising abruptly behind: this assemblage of nature and construction seemed to *mean* something, to be symbolizing, or even saying something profound and timeless, and also seemed to have always been there just like that because it could not be any other way.

Greece is a stage. The famous clarity of the light there—you can see the contours and depth of a small hill four miles away—makes it a beautifully illuminated stage. That must be why drama was invented there, and why the first masterpieces of the theater were Greek.

The light had one other quality; it seemed to be right. In many parts of the world the light didn't look right; it seemed to be bleaching the colors, for example, or blurring contours, or making things look garish, and it tended to have correspondingly distorting effect on your feelings, making you vaguely depressed without reason, or a little disturbed or a little shrill. But in Greece the light was right.

But as I said, the food was mediocre. You either liked Greece or you didn't. You either liked the wail of the music or you didn't. We sat down at one of the rough tables. "I *like* that music," Gloria said.

Men were sitting at the other tables, and the women were gathered by themselves in a corner. This was the semi-Orient, they were respectable women: they did not dance in public. No one was drinking much; hardly anyone ever drank very much. The women wore simple cotton dresses and had their hair frizzed in the style of the 1930's; the men, naturally without coats in the summer heat, went in for more contrast. One young man had on a pair of chocolate brown slacks, black shirt, silver necktie, black and white striped socks, and large white shoes. He had a lot of hair and a long pencil mustache over his wide, white constant smile. Another man, older, undersized, in purple shirt and blue pants, got up to dance by himself. As he took the floor he looked as though he was unhappy and a failure. And then he began to dance to the sensual music, and suddenly over his tired face there came a charmed, slow smile, and into his thin body came a swaying, pumping grace; out of this middle-aged man emerged a happy faun, moving with a slow and easy passion, with a kind of knowledgeability, a worldliness. It was uncanny. Where had he developed this range, what was it based on, how could he possess this much inner grace?

He must have found it in the music, developed it from the dance, from the tradition of the two in Greece. It was a gift of culture, a Greek's way of releasing what was inside of him, dancing instead of drinking.

The man with the silver necktie took the floor. Arms extended, hands hanging down and snapping up, he danced with his head down, concentrating on some spot on the floor, advancing toward it, drawing back, circling it, trying so it seemed by every means to win it, charm, hypotize it. He danced for about five minutes without ever repeating himself, without noticing the people around him, who weren't noticing him either; the only relationship now was between the dancer and the spot on the floor. At last he seemed satisfied; he had communicated whatever it was. There was naturally no applause. He hadn't been dancing for anyone else; no one had paid much attention. He went back to his table and took a sip of wine.

The *taverna* was getting more and more animated as the night grew later, its shabbiness fading further into the background. We were sitting outdoors at wooden tables in the dirt. The dancers were performing on a concrete floor in front of the *taverna,* with a couple of naked bulbs above them for illumination, aided by the clear Grecian moon sliced into the star-crowded sky. Just beyond our table was the water of the Aegean—black glass—and across it, a few hundred yards away, the Peloponnesus reared its black mountains against the sky.

The proprietor, tall, fat, middle-aged, got up to dance with his barefoot three-year-old daughter. It was now one o'clock in the morning. What was she doing up at this hour? Why, dancing; Daddy was teaching her to dance. The proprietor transformed himself the moment he started dancing into a kind of bisexual Arabian houri, all swaying shoulders and slowly swiveling hips, face set in a slow, concentrated smile, all the while encouraging the tiny girl below his belly. She was not able to follow the steps he was doing very well, but something of the sensual quality of the dance was beginning to come into her body.

Very late that night I fell asleep in my bunk aboard the *Toscana* in the port of Poros, and at dawn was awakened by a crash, as though a tower of dishes had collapsed. We were at sea again, and it was rough. We were being bluntly notified that "yachting" wasn't the same thing as going for a car ride in the mountains, nor was it like a golfing holiday, or two weeks at the shore; it was committing yourself to the sea, and the sea was a monster. Tracing our route from island to island beforehand on a map I did not comprehend that that blue part my finger so easily moved across was a wilderness completely controlled by two savages, wind and water. The *Toscana* swiveled slowly in an eccentric roll-and-pitch as I tried to fall asleep again. But every time I opened my eyes the walls of my little cabin looked unreal and oppressive, as though they formed the chamber for some advanced and unnatural scientific experiment, testing weightlessness perhaps, their weird angles and planes seemed to me, in the new slang sense of the word, sick. I hurriedly got up, pulled on a bathing suit, and went up on deck. As soon as my eye fell on the horizon, vast and immobile, the world was all right again.

The stern of the *Toscana* was rising up and sinking like a haywire elevator, the bow plunging its nose into the sea like an animal. A very odd wind went hissing unstoppably across the sunny blue water. It was very strong and unnaturally steady, a great blast continuously pushing against the *Toscana.* It made the sea's surface a complete field of agitated water, like a million frantically bobbing needles. This wind was the baleful *meltemi,* the "bad wind" which howls down from the Black Sea and through the center of the Aegean off and on throughout the summer.

A great wave from the starboard side rolled menacingly up and smashed against the side of the ship, drenching me. I retreated inside the deck cabin, and soon all nine of us were there, waiting.

Henry announced, "The captain says we can't make the upper end of Amorgos island in this sea, so we're going around the lower end, and then along the coast to the port. It's a very small port. They have no radio, so we can't ask them what the sea is like there. The captain says he hopes we can get into it. There's nowhere else to put in."

That was becoming plain. We were coming up along the coast of Amorgos now; it was impenetrable, a high rugged gray cliff of rock stretching into the distance. No hint of an inlet or beach, no sign of life anywhere; meanwhile the bizarre gale roared at us in the happy sunshine. The sea was now a bright purple. Occasionally the pitch and roll of the *Toscana* became too much for something below decks, which broke loose with a bang or a crash. The gale, coming from the starboard—from the island side—pressed irresistibly against the *Toscana,* like a hand wrestler forcing his opponent slowly, implacably over, further, a little further. The waves continued to roll up and explode against the tarpaulin-protected windows of the deck cabin. We sat tight inside, pitching in our camp chairs. If the ship got into serious trouble we could not get off her. The lifeboat could not be launched in this sea, and of course even the best swimmer would have been drowned in a few minutes wallowing against the gale blowing him away from the island.

We could only sit and wait, which we did in the way we thought best. That is, we were rather silent and calm on the outside. Occasionally someone would say something funny or almost funny; the others would laugh. We belonged to the culture of Northern Europe transplanted to America, and so knew we had to stay calm in a crisis. It was valuable knowledge, because a burst of alarm from any of them would have made me even more scared, and I knew that they were in the same condition. So we all sat looking serenely into space, silent, until someone would say, "Deck tennis, anyone?" and then we would laugh, and then a calm silence would follow.

This kind of "Anglo-Saxon" emotional control has won battles, crushed mutinies, faced down tyrants, and won through many other storms in history; it is splendid in a storm. The only trouble is that most of life isn't a storm at all, and this control can make all the rest of life on the drab side, produce misunderstandings between people, chill humanity and be a great fertilizer for hypocrites. Right now, though, pitching in my camp chair in a savage sea, I saw its strength.

If there hadn't been so much sunshine it wouldn't have seemed so dangerous. A gale as strong as this on a completely cloudless day was so far from anything I'd known that I felt anything else was also possible: a dragon on the cliffs breathing fire, for instance.

The captain lurched into the cabin, said he had been studying the charts and that the port of Amorgos was our sole possible harbor, looked rather dubious, and made his way back to the wheelhouse.

Against the rearing gray wall of cliff I suddenly noticed something incredible. In the midst of that lifeless, desolate waste I saw a great white slab high on the face of the cliff above the sea, a Shangri-La, a soaring whitewashed facade held against the sheer rock by white buttresses and broken by a strange pattern of windows. "What in the world—?"

"Monastery," said Michaelis, the steward.

Seeing it made our present isolation somehow more intense. There it was; people lived in it. Here we were; nothing and no one could reach us. The space and emptiness of the Aegean were not then the surcease they had seemed, but an elemental threat instead. The banality of, for instance, Long Island Sound, crowded and surrounded by all the paraphernalia of the twentieth century, didn't look so banal any more; the overstuffed life in the United States of America had its compensations after all. It was safe. We had gone, on a yacht to be sure, but still gone Back to Nature, forgetting that nature was half evil. That half howled all around us now. The fundamental question had to present itself at last: had I gone too far into the Aegean and into life itself and committed the classic error of *hubris*—going beyond the natural limits of my nature—for which I would now pay the classic consequences, tragedy? In this brilliant, towering storm, it seemed a sound question.

If this was *hubris,* Henry's response was Bacchus. "Michaelis!" he suddenly cried, "*Ouzo!* Scotch! Ice!" And by a feat of balancing, Michaelis succeeded in carrying the bottles and glasses up to us from the galley, and with much spilling and splashing we managed to pass around these refreshments. Then we settled back a little more philosophically to let nature, which was going to anyway, take its course.

This wild afternoon ended when the *Toscana,* superficially a shambles, the decks covered with a wreckage of glass and food and clothes, plunged at last into the port of Amorgos, a large circle of sheltered, smooth blue water. At the center of the harbor, straight ahead of us, there was a green, tree-crowded promontory supporting a brilliantly white Byzantine church of many arches, with two white bell towers beside it, each with two levels of arches and a silver dome; the church itself had a much larger silver dome. On either side of this strange and beautiful building and separated from it by empty land, there were two small white groups of houses, and behind it all rose bare billowing hills. Here again was the extraordinary drama of Greek landscape combined with buildings, looking not only beautiful but also inevitable; it had to be this way, in accordance with some inevitable plan and meaning. For us, of course, the meaning of the port of Amorgos that afternoon was clear. We were safe again.

It seemed good for the nerves to face elemental danger and escape from it. For so long the physical dangers facing me had been the stale city ones: getting trapped in an elevator or run over by a truck, or beaten up by disturbed city youths while walking home late at night, which was just as stale, artificial and unnatural a danger as the first two. These exacerbated young characters were just as much a waste product of the city as the grime on the buildings: there they were in the street, hopelessly overstimulated by all the hucksters and entertainers and salesmen of America but with no way of getting at all these stimulants. And so they became stimulants themselves, violent ones.

But now these victims were far away and so was the kind of jangled, dry danger they represented. I had just ridden out a major gale in a very small ship, and was now drifting safely across this halcyon harbor.

After such a day, we naturally set off the next morning to pay a visit to the monastery. Its name was the Monastery of the Presentation of Our Lady, and it contained a famous Broken Icon. We hired donkeys and zigzagged for an hour up a rocky way to the height of the island, creaking along on a wooden seat sidesaddle, the muleteers walking along beside and the sun fixing its hottest point squarely on the back of my neck, creaking upward slowly until we came to the main stairway of the hill town, which was called as usual the Chora, being greeted by housewives and children from white balconies on both sides of the stairway, being, almost, applauded, for our prowess on donkeyback perhaps, or simply because we were foreigners. In Greek there are two main words describing attitudes toward foreigners: "xenophobe," foreigner-hating; and "xenophile," foreigner-loving. You hear "xenophile" very often. ("The reason we love foreigners," a Greek told me, darkly, "is that we hate each other.") In English we have only borrowed "xenophobe."

We paused under a grape arbor to drink some cold soda and then creaked slowly on, beginning to descend the other side of the island, down the cliff face we had battered our way past yesterday; a thousand feet below, the brilliant blue sea that had done the battering spread itself quietly under the sunshine, and the path here became a rigid back-and-forth descent, where a misstep by my donkey would have dropped both of us into the sea. But he seemed sure-footed enough, and so I stayed on in the saddle for another hour as we descended the cliff to within a few hundred feet of the sea and then began to zigzag upward again around a rock spur. On the other side of it I saw the monastery above me, fastened to the face of the cliff, white and thin, like a tombstone, perhaps ten stories high and one small room wide.

I wonder if we should have come, I asked myself not for the first or last time in Greece. Was there any building in the world which tried harder to be solitary? Hadn't they gone to almost superhuman trouble to be alone? And still here we were, trailing up on our asses. Well, here we were, and it was not the sort of situation for remarking, "I think I'll skip this one and wait for you across the street," so I got off in the little white courtyard, walked up the short flight of steps and ducked through the doorway—a very low one, Keep Out—up the white inner staircase, one wall of which was the monastery and the other was the cliff, up to a blue, curtained, unreal, lacy little parlor. An emaciated, shabby monk asked us with a sweet smile to sit down around a circular wooden table. He seemed to welcome us genuinely, but there was the sense that he would have just as genuinely welcomed our not coming. Large brown photographs of bearded, hatted, chain-wearing patriarchs of the Orthodox Church hung on the walls. The young monk with his thin beard looked like a completely wrung-dry version of them. He brought us liqueur and Turkish coffee. His gray cassock had been carefully patched many times, and he wore a little black skullcap. The other monks joined us one by one. There were five of them living here, always. Two were about thirty years old, two were middle-aged, and all of these reflected the poverty and emaciation of the first who had greeted us. The fifth monk, however, was magnificently venerable, rather short and wide, and glorified by a splendid, spreading, curling white beard: St. Nicholas he seemed, a radiant presence in his workroom, his silver head gleaming in the Aegean sunlight. All of them seemed welcoming in an impersonal sense. They conducted us to the chapel, which was above the parlor, a small room with big bulbous silver chandeliers hanging from the ceiling in front of the altar screen. Icons, the two-dimensional holy pictures of Orthodoxy, covered the screen, and were themselves almost hidden under elaborately worked gold and silver plate laid over the painting. The famous Broken Icon, a Madonna and Child heavily plated in gold and silver and with the two figures wearing jeweled crowns, hung next to the screen. It had come here in centuries past in an unmanned boat from Cyprus, accompanied by only a lighted lamp, to escape desecration. It was cracked horizontally in two places. There was here and in the chapel and in the parlor below and everywhere in the monastery a feeling that some key bolt holding it fastened to the cliff might suddenly give way and the whole thing would go sliding and crashing down to the rocks below and into the sea. This sense of precariousness seemed an effective symbol of what life is ultimately like, not only its physical dangers but its spiritual pits: surely anyone living in the Monastery of the Presentation of Our Lady would instinctively aspire *upward,* with those rocks and that sea, like death, waiting so directly below them always. Five Greek men lived their lives here as hermits, for no organized monastic community life of course was possible for so few. As I stood looking at the Broken Icon, one of the muleteers went by me out onto the little balcony opening off the chapel. He was the other, predominant kind of Greek: that is, there was a large bell in a little tower there, and so he began to ring it. In Greece, if you see a bell, ring it; if you see a flower, admire it or pick it; if you see an opportunity to make love, take it. The bell pealed out into the vast spaces of air above the Aegean, out along the great empty rock cliff, a startling clang in all the silence. One of the monks moved past me to the balcony, and gently asked the man to stop. The muleteer shrugged and let go of the bell rope. It had been fun while it lasted.

We put an offering of money in a little box in a corner of the chapel, and signed the guest book. Ex-Queen Soraya of Iran had been one of the few recent visitors. So had a M. Georges Gapp of Lille, France. Beside his name he noted that his visit had been *"par hasard."* How could he or anyone come to the Monastery of the Presentation of Our Lady "by chance"? There was the empty sea and the desolation of rock on all sides. Had he been shipwrecked, or fallen out of an airplane?

Afterward we passed out of this Byzantine world of the Orthodox faith with its sixteen hundred years of history in Greece, past all the centuries and the icons and the patriarchs, into the Greece of gods and oracles and temples, which reached without interruption another thousand years or so into the past.

There was nothing "timeless" about Greece. Everything had a rather definite place on the ladder of past time and that was why it seemed accessible to us, why we could imagine something of what it was like, why its reality was still so strong. There had been many changes but no interruption between what Homer described in the *Odyssey,* what Odysseus saw and did on his voyage and what we were seeing and doing now, two thousand eight hundred years later. It was all connected. The Greek people understood this and took it as an unremarkable matter of course: on

Samos they still often talked of Pythagoras, their native son who had made good and done them proud; on Cos the people practically knew Hippocrates personally and thought he was fine, although a slight bore by now; and on Delos, the core and jewel of all these islands, they would have waved Apollo himself out into the open except that they had all been killed, and so finally Apollo had died there too of neglect.

No American is ever placed in time with this kind of Greek certainty. The past of an American trails back a few generations and then must make the leap across an ocean and lose itself in a vague earlier family history in one or two or three or four old countries somewhere. Perhaps that is one reason we are comparatively energetic, feeling that we have to build a total world in America by ourselves. In Greece they knew that they had been there for thousands of years and that everything was likely to go on and on and on. They couldn't wait to come to us, to America, where they would be energetic too, and hoped to make lots of money, but then they wanted to go back to Greece, to home, family, to continuity.

Delos was dead, beautiful and strange. The wind of the Aegean swept over its few acres, slid around its one physical feature, little Mount Cynthos, drifted among the fields of ruined palaces and temples and theaters, and touched no stir of life anywhere.

Coming up to the island by boat was tricky, because of this wind. We approached along a narrow and shifting channel between Delos and the island of Reneia. Two reefs cut the surface of this channel, and there was a strange sea running, a brilliantly blue and subtly difficult sea. Little rocky peninsulas of the island reached into the channel, and around them the water was a glowing, luminous green. Across it all the capricious wind of the Aegean swept now in one direction, soon in another, brushing up silver on the surface of the sea and ruffling the weeds of the island. Everywhere there was movement and shifting colors and changing currents and doubt. Only the wrecked monuments of Apollo stood immovable at the center of all the flux; and at the center of the center there was a broken, awkward stump of a once-great statue of him, powerfully carved in white marble, a part of the torso and legs, twenty-five hundred years old.

We disembarked and started into this sanctuary. Delos is three miles long, less than one mile wide. It is greenish-brown now, and there are very few trees. Mount Cynthos, the towering climax of the island from which Zeus watched the birth of Apollo, is just 368 feet high. Except for the statue of Apollo, which must have been huge, everything about Delos is rather small and careful, on the scale of humans. Taste or harmony or balance or common sense dominated what was made here. The central square, the Sacred Way, the Sacred Lake, the amphitheater, the Temple of Apollo itself were not awe-inspiring. The awe was apparently supposed to come from Apollo; from his shrines there only came beauty. Even the Delian lions are about the size of real lions, which they only somewhat resemble. Archaically carved in white marble, seated on their haunches, their long rib-showing bodies tense, mouths gaping, they have confronted the wind of Delos for twenty-six hundred years and been wind-changed to the sleekness of sea lions, roaring still through worn-away heads. They face across the Sacred Lake, which is dry now of course—all the Apollonian waters everywhere are dry—and full of rushes and a few palm trees. Behind it there is a little museum, where many very beautiful statues and fragments have been gathered from around the island. Next to the museum there is a small guest house, the only other non-ruin on Delos.

Few visitors were there this summer day, and no guide was in evidence. Gloria Etting and I ventured along toward Mount Cynthos. She was taking pictures. We passed the smallish amphitheater, its central half-circle of stage restored, with a trough circling beneath it where rainwater flowing down the bank of stone seats was caught and led into a subterranean cistern. Weeds grew among the semicircle of seats, and soil had flowed down and carried away the upper rows.

She stopped to take some pictures, and I wandered on through the remains of Hellenic houses, rooms opening on a colonnade which surrounded a central, roofless court. Usually there was a mosaic on the floor of the courtyard, perhaps a beautiful dolphin in green, blue and white, or an elegant, stylized, Modern-Art-like black and white abstract, a Picasso-like man with a flute, a splendidly stylized trident, a gorgeous panther with Dionysos riding on his back. Near one house there was a well, God knows how old. A man came up with a wooden pail, opened the well and drew some water; so Delos wasn't bone-dry after all. He gave me a drink; it was very cold and good, and very few things are as good as something cold to drink in Greece outdoors at noon in the summer. I threaded on through the narrow turning way, past the walls of these two-thousand-years-old homes, and at a corner found Gloria again. "I went into that temple," she indicated a classical marble structure the size of an important living room, "to take a picture of that statue, the woman's figure with the beautiful drapery. Who is she?"

"She's the Egyptian goddess Isis."

"And from every direction lizards ran out at me. 'Get the hell out of here' is what they were saying, 'Get the hell out of here with your camera.' I never got the picture."

" 'The lizards of Delos,' " I read, " 'were believed to be descended from the crocodiles of Egypt.' "

She blinked and then laughed.

We continued a little higher up barren Mount Cynthos. The higher we went the more the wind on this bright sunny day cut at us. We were entirely alone, and the going was rather steep up this rocky path.

"Look at that pink marble," she said as we passed a wall. "Stand next to it while I take a picture, will you? To give the scale."

I took my place, and then suddenly realized that I didn't want to have my picture taken, not because I was there only as a human measuring rod but because I felt completely out of place. I was wearing a semi-cowboy outfit, semi-dungarees and T-shirt, and a kind of army fatigue cap, practical for roaming over the Aegean islands in the summer, but raw and crude and sloppy to wear and be photographed in among the small and careful and ancient perfections of Delos, even Delos in ruins.

Nevertheless she took the picture, and we were proceeding a little higher when an unreal din suddenly broke out below us, deep cries, roaring and croaking, cries, voices, loud, crude, blaring. "What in the world—?"

Two white doves suddenly flew out of nowhere and passed over.

Motionless with surprise, I didn't say anything for a moment and then blurted, "Frogs, it's frogs."

"Oh. Yes, of course, frogs. I never heard frogs as loud as those."

"Neither have I."

"And I never heard frogs sound as human as those."

"Neither have I." And then I added, "They scared those two white doves, which is why they suddenly flew over."

"They're the only birds I've seen on Delos."

"Yes."

She said, "Shall we go on to the top?"

After a few steps, Gloria said, "I suppose here begins the most sacred part of the island."

"Probably about here, yes."

We were both frankly suspicious that there just might be some—some Thing still in a niche or a cave or an altar somewhere. Everything was so unsettled and unsettling, the shifting currents and changeable colors in the sea around us, that peculiar, unnatural-seeming wind, the *smallness* of it all, the uncanny feeling of tragedy, the sense of dignity violated and integrity debased. It seemed just possible that the outrages committed against Delos might have left some power behind, some phantom raised up by all the grief.

Staying with each other, we went on to the summit of Mount Cynthos. There was a pedestal, some rubble—nothing else living or dead.

The sea, deeply blue except for the glowing green pool in which Delos floated, stretched far away into the mist, where the faint but formidable outlines of much larger islands hovered on all sides—Andros, Syros, Tenos, Mykonos, Naxos, Paros—forming a circle around the tiny hub of Delos. These were the Cyclades, the Circle, and there was another ring of islands outside these inner seven. The Cyclades occupy the center of the Aegean, halfway from Greece to Asia Minor, and in ancient times their power was considerable and their strategic importance tremendous.

Looking from the horizon down on Delos I could see the ivory-colored temples, the white pillars, the pink walls, the lovely miniature ruins of the ancient Delos of Apollo. Far down another slope there was a small, circular threshing floor, and six horses were being driven around it like the hands of a clock. A little growing was being done here now, but the people who did it lived on Mykonos. Nobody has tried to live on Delos for a very long time.

Delos had everything. First of all, it was the birthplace of Apollo, the god of light, beauty, intellect, art, music, and poetry, who was the link between the world and the other gods, the god the Greeks loved most, embodying their ideal of manhood, the symbol of their spirit of reason and measure, Apollo the Beautiful, Apollo Who Spoke. Delos became his sacred sanctuary some time before history began. In the fifth century B.C., to heighten the island's purity, all the dead bodies were dug up and moved away, and no one afterwards was allowed to die or be born on Delos. An unexpected sudden death had to be followed by elaborate purification ceremonies. Pilgrims from all parts of the Hellenic world came to Delos for the great festivals to Apollo with gifts for the god's treasury, with money to build still another temple or another palace; the Delian citizens themselves, rich and cosmopolitan, erected still more theaters and public buildings and shrines and monuments. The festivals increased in ambitious splendor every year, with elaborate competitions in music and dancing and poetry, with horse races and theater, the Athenian contingent arriving once by a glittering bridge thrown across from the island of Reneia. Many nationalities established themselves and their gods and their art on Delos under the protection of Apollo. At the beginning of the fifth century B.C. the Persians swept through the Cyclades, invading right and left, but keeping a respectful distance away from sacred Delos.

As if this spiritual preeminence and artistic richness weren't enough, tiny Delos began to demonstrate a strong talent for commerce. It had the last good, small but good, harbor before Asia Minor, and since it was impervious to the turmoil of wars or pirates, traders by the thousands made their headquarters there. More riches rained down on this island three miles long; by the second century B.C. it was one of the greatest commercial centers of the Mediterranean.

And then time began to run out for Delos, as it was running out for Greek civilization. Time began to overtake even Apollo, who had held sway for so long over the minds and destiny of Hellas. Apollo was a god, but he was not immortal; he lived on belief, and belief was growing weak.

In 88 B.C., during a war between Rome and Mithridates of Pontus, the latter suddenly struck at Delos, so extremely rich, so traditionally defenseless, and after all vaguely allied with the enemy, Rome. It was a sacrilege, but could Apollo really defend himself, avenge himself? Twenty thousand people were slaughtered in a day, and nothing was left standing on the island.

The next year the Romans retook it, for even after such a thoroughgoing sacking Delos retained its good harbor and perhaps some vestiges of its spiritual authority. The Romans patched it all up as best they could, succeeding to the point where Delos once again began to look tempting. So pirates swept down in 69 B.C., destroying everything, stealing everything and taking the people as slaves. The Romans, nothing if not persevering, at long last decided to build defenses on Delos.

But there was no longer anything much to defend. Neighbors began sailing over to carry off some of the marvelous marble for building on their own islands. Athens was by now the "protector" of Delos, but there was nothing of any practical use there any more, just ruined beauty, just history. The island was put up for auction. There were no takers.

Nothing further has happened to it during the last two thousand years, except for work by archaeologists recently. The Mykonots use it as a sheep run.

And Apollo? In the fourth century A.D. the Roman Emperor Julian the Apostate, trying to turn Rome back from its new Christianity to the old gods, sent a famous doctor,

Oribasius, to Apollo's other great shrine, Delphi, on the mainland of Greece. From it had come the great oracular pronouncements that for centuries had rung through the Greek world. In the depths of a great temple a priestess sitting on a tripod, and aided it is believed by a mysterious vapor and a sacred spring and a sacred laurel tree, would go into an ecstatic seizure and babble out the answer to a suppli-cant's question. The heroes and rulers of Greece had trooped to her; war, life, everything hung on her poetic, ambiguous pronouncements, for she was the earthly voice of Apollo.

So Julian's doctor went to Delphi and brought back to the Emperor this message, the last, heartbroken words ever spoken by the oracle: "Tell the Emperor that the bright cita-del has fallen to the ground; Apollo has no longer any shelter, or oracular laurel tree, or a spring that speaks; even the vocal stream has ceased to flow."

But there was one more hope. There is a tradition that Julian himself came to desolate Delos and climbed Mount Cynthos to implore a message, a sign, from Apollo; but there was nothing to be seen there, and only silence from Apollo on the summit of Mount Cynthos, or more likely only the hiss of the Aegean wind. The Christians were relieved; Apollo had been a manifestation of the Devil.

We started down the rocky path from Mount Cynthos, down through the intricately winding little streets, the tiny squares, the open courtyards, past the House of the Trident and the House of Dionysos, the markets and sanctuaries and pools, down toward the Sacred Way and the little spur of land where our boat was waiting.

The poignancy of wrecked beauty was everywhere: in the courtyard of a weedy palace with the mosaic as bright and alive as ever and all else worn and time-changed beyond imagining; a husband and wife in white marble, her robe draped with the grace of flying water, standing without heads in the devastation of their home; a colonnaded street with all the pillars broken; and most of all the sense still of bustle and prosperity, of full, busy houses all now facelessly ended, done for thousands of years ago. On every side the wreckage evoked their confidence and their accomplishments, the great underground cistern and its row of stone arches holding intact still today, and even water at the bottom, sickly green, with a frog floating on it. During the great contests of music and singing at the festivals of Apollo, Delos had been awash with melodic voices and the vibrance of strings; the silence there now was like an alarming vacuum, like the silence which follows the abrupt cessation of a great orchestra playing in an empty hall; ruined, the stump of Apollo in white alive marble was awkwardly propped up, like some terrible relic of a saint's body, grotesquely preserved. Delos was the gutted light of ancient Greece, at the mercy of every passing wind, of any traveler with itchy fingers, of any stray goat.

"Do you know something?" Gloria said as we got near the familiar yacht in which we had been sailing the Aegean for weeks. "I was just a little nervous for a while as we were going up Mount Cynthos."

"Yes."

"I can't explain it. There's something funny about this island, something—incomplete, like an interrupted scream."

We were almost at the gangplank now, with all the home-like reassurance that it offered.

"After all," she went on, "there's nothing whatever on this poor little place to be nervous about."

"Nothing except getting old and then older and then so old that you're vulnerable to everything."

Delos inspired no other fear, except perhaps the fear that what I thought great and eternal and true in life might also be growing old, might some day sicken and die and be forgotten too; that our life today in other words might be meaningless.

From Delos to Athos is a rather long sea passage north through the Aegean. It is the passage from the sunlit, sensuous world of Apollo to the darkened celibate caves of hermit Christianity a thousand years later. That was the difference that millennium of disaster made spiritually in the Greek people.

Athos, first of all, looks the antithesis of ravaged Delos: it is all fertility, crowded with ripe green forests and fields, flowing and flowering and alive. Yet of the two it is Delos which gives the impression of having been, once, marvelously vital, while Athos for all its fertility has a certain brittle hollowness about it, as though it were a wonderfully lifelike plaster church statue, everything there except the pulse.

It too seemed haunted, much more so than Delos where the ghosts had all given up ages ago; here they cling on, as though whining around the foggy flanks of the mountain, tenaciously clinging, strung gaping across the rich forests.

As we approached it the crystal light of the Aegean dimmed; a vague purplish-gray mist and cloud bank flowed out from the land until where the sky ended and the horizon began could no longer be made out, nor where the land ended and the sea began: all became like one huge screen, everything in front of us and around us shaded together into a featureless, sunless haze of light gray, and we sailed along in a world of silent, painted-sea unreality.

The peninsula of Mount Athos is twenty-five miles long, and averages about three miles wide. It is one of three parallel peninsulas extending southeast from the mainland of northern Greece, pointing toward Turkey. Finally we began to make it out, a jagged range culminating in the Holy Mountain, more than six thousand feet high, which dropped steeply down to the Aegean, forming one of the most troublesome capes for sailors in the Mediterranean. It was here that the famous destruction in a storm of the Persian armada sailing down upon seemingly doomed Greece took place in 492 B.C. There was still very often some kind of storm here. On the very high and steep cliffs above the fatal stretch of sea men dedicated to God have lived alone in caves for a thousand years.

There were long, thin tongues of whiteness in protected gorges on the mountainside, now in midsummer, in Greece, in the Aegean, and after a long argument the fact was established that they were snow; they were like banners proclaiming that the lightness and warmth and clarity associated with Greece did not include this particular part of it.

We continued along the green shore of the peninsula to its sole port, Daphne, and anchored at a large rusted iron buoy. It was about noon, and the sun at last began to creep out. Ten or twelve decrepit buildings made up the port, some of them half-timbered, with frail wooden balconies; there was one short, rough cobbled street, and a few monks and a few soldiers all in a state of reverie or apathy. The men in our party went ashore at this hamlet, and found it in all essentials still the world of the Byzantine Empire, which ended in 1453, the obscure Eastern version of the Middle Ages.

Mount Athos was about to celebrate the thousandth anniversary of its founding; the first modern road had been cut into it to transport the King of Greece, the Patriarch of Constantinople, and hundreds of others who would arrive for the observance in a few days. Dozens of cars would be landed, and even now there was one large work truck at Daphne, and we were given transportation in it, the raw road snaking up the mountainside through groves of olive trees and cypresses until we reached the top of the ridge, at two thousand feet, where the big truck began to plunge very fast and heavily into an interior valley stuffed with gardens and trees and flowers and hills and vines and hedges, and strewn with villas and palaces and monasteries and churches, towers and turrets and domes and walls, all of it overhung with the serenity of a millennium of contemplation, the stillness of places where engines had never been. This blaring and clanging truck was setting up vibrations Athos had never known before; it plunged on past drowsing orange-roofed villas crowded by gardens and shrubbery, until we reached the floor of the valley and the "capital" of Mount Athos, the village of Karyes. There the driver established for the first time that the truck had brakes: he stopped, and we climbed unsteadily down, into Byzantium again.

We went along the narrow and stony streets in the sun, past the half-timbered projecting houses of the Middle Ages, past a small café with rough wooden tables, a vast Russian monastery, the mansion of the Greek Government's representative—Mount Athos is a theocratic republic under the protection of Greece—and the entire dreaming town seemed completely implausible, even impossible. It was one thing for a monastery to be entirely male, but Mount Athos was a very sizable stretch of country with much agriculture and produce and some commerce, and no woman had been permitted to set foot on it for nine hundred years. That fact gave it an inexplicable, uncanny feeling. How could a way of life be generated here for so long when not so much as a cow or a hen, let alone a woman, had been allowed? It seemed some ancient and ponderous trick of balance, like a big house standing on one corner. Buildings could be celibate, but fields and woods, lots of them, mile after mile of coastline, a mountain chain, two towns? Uncanny and brittle, the atmosphere of Athos percolated through all the abundant natural life springing up on all sides and gave no answer. How?

"Faith," said a husky old monk with a round gray beard and a Theodore-Roosevelt manner of impatient energy, "with faith one can do everything. And without faith? Why, without faith, one can do nothing, of course. Everyone knows that is so." I asked myself if I believed that that was so. Faith.

Access to Mount Athos by "any woman, female animal, child, eunuch, or person with beardless face" was prohibited by Emperor Constantine Monomachos of Byzantium in 1060. The wild peninsula was already a haven for holy solitaries, and the first monastery had been organized in 963. Then followed a history of more and more monasteries being built, until there were forty in all, and countless hermits living alone, and others living in small communities of houses called *skites,* monks coming to spend their lives at Athos from all over the Orthodox world—Serbs and Bulgarians and Slavs and Russians and Greeks and other Christians from Asia Minor and North Africa. Great holdings of land began to accrue to the monasteries in all these countries, and money and glittering gifts from emperors rolled in. There were pirate raids and monasteries burned down, and in the middle of the fifteenth century the Turks captured Constantinople and seized the Byzantine Empire, including Greece. This event, which was a catastrophe everywhere else in Greece, left Athos in all essentials miraculously unaffected, proving its uniqueness, and its strangeness.

None of this history, however, meant very much because Mount Athos was timeless, or close to it: time, when it was noticed at all, was Byzantine Time. Time was not important. *God have mercy on us, God have mercy on us;* through the nights for a thousand years hundreds of thousands of men millions of times repeated *God have mercy on us,* and God being outside time they strove also to escape from it, so that Mount Athos, like God, would have no history.

They usually prayed together for eight noncontinuous hours a day, beginning soon after midnight, with much longer services for special holy days. They ate little food normally and much less during fasting periods. Mass, vespers, complines, night service, vigils, always they were worshiping or just had worshiped or were just about to worship God.

We continued along through the ethereal atmosphere of Karyes up to the wide marble steps of the Council Building. At five in the afternoon, Western Time, a monk began calling the Elders representing all the monasteries of Athos to Council by beating rhythmically with a mallet on a long slab of shaped wood, the *simandron:* it came into being because one of the few Turkish regulations enforced on Mount Athos was the prohibition of bells. From various corners of town the Elders in their black cassocks, flat-topped black hats, beards, uncut hair knotted up in back, sometimes with chains of office around their necks and carrying patriarchal staffs, slowly and singly converged on the Council Chamber.

There they approved our applications to visit Athos, and we set off by foot from this central valley of the peninsula down to the opposite coast from where we had landed, and the tenth century monastery of Iveron. The rocky, dusty path led fairly steeply into an Arcadian valley full of still beauty, the late afternoon sun behind us flooding all along it, illuminating sprays of olive trees and cypresses with a still, glowing perfection, something Leonardo da Vinci only might have faithfully painted; hanging in the air was the smell of broom and Spanish chestnuts, of wild flowers and leaves, and there was an undertone of bees in unison, and strangest of all a superabundance of water, in Greece: here and everywhere on Mount Athos, water, springs, brooks, the element Greeks break their hearts for lack of elsewhere flowed all around us here. Instead of sad little driblets around some failing plant in cracked soil there were everywhere here silver slides of water, held in big mountainside cisterns above the rooftops, or flowing steadily into a trough, or spraying out of a conduit, spreading in all directions, lots of it, lots of clear cool water. We walked on down this spell-struck valley, through the Mediterranean pines and the olive groves and the earth smells and the feel of moisture until at the bottom of it, close to the sea, we came to a vast solitary barracks of a place, its featureless stone foundation raising it perhaps forty feet high; and perched on top were two stories which had once been painted yellow but were now stripped of color: Iveron Monastery.

It was not yet quite sunset, so the gates had not been closed for the night. Two monks gravely greeted us in the cobbled forecourt and led us through a huge portal and a high, brightly painted tunnel into the big central courtyard, with grass thinly creeping over the paving stones, and across it to a corner of the monastery where visitors were lodged. On the walls of a determined little reception room were portraits of the Russian Czars Peter the Great, Alexander II, and Nicholas II, and even Edward VII of England, whose connection with Greek Orthodoxy seemed to be only that his cousins, the Romanovs of Russia, were Orthodox. In any case there they all were, the old monarchs, and with the death of the last of them, Nicholas II, eliminated in the Siberian cellar in 1918, Mount Athos began to die also, for no more monks, and no more revenues, of course came from the new Soviet Russia; when Orthodox Bulgaria and Yugoslavia became Communist after the Second World War the paralysis of Athos spread further. On this peninsula where forty thousand monks had lived, lived in a sense splendidly, amid flourishing art and scholarship, there were about fifteen hundred of them left, rattling around in the vast establishments, thirty-five in a monastery meant for five hundred, or eighty in a monastery meant for a thousand. Some now were learned most were not at all; some now were young, most were very old.

We had supper at a long wooden table with two other visitors, a round elderly German who was writing a book, and a French schoolteacher who was translating a manuscript. For light, an acetylene lamp hissed on the mantelpiece. Supper was a kind of *pasta* in oil, two sardines, bread, and strong Athos red wine. It was certainly as much, perhaps more, than the monks got.

Then we went along the huge empty stone corridors, here and there an acetylene lamp relieving the blackness, the monks scattered around the huge old place, tucked away in towers and corners, others living in little farmhouses up the valley, still and snug now in the moonlight—they were responsible for part of the uncanniness of Athos, those celibate farmhouses. We went upstairs to a large room with half a dozen beds in it, the long windows looking down onto the pines and olives far below. We were high above everything on the huge foundation. Across the corridor there was a little old wooden balcony fixed to the face of the building, as impermanent-looking as a fly on the wall; balconies like it were an Athos architectural habit, to symbolize perhaps the fleeting quality of life. At nine we went to bed, which was a wooden board covered with a mat.

At four we were awakened for the service. The monks had been in church, as usual, since 12:30 A.M. We walked to it across the courtyard and found the church almost completely black. Going in, there were only a few candles and altar lamps touching off reflections on silver and marble and brass surfaces. New and old and very old incense was heavily in the air. We found our way into high narrow wooden stalls with the seats folded back so that you couldn't exactly sit in them. Slowly the church emerged a little from the blackness.

We were seated along the back wall. In front of us, about

twenty feet away, was the wall called the iconostasis, which separated the body of the church from the altar. The icons hung on it, and in the center there was a doorway partially filled by two small doors. Behind them was the altar, a table with a domed top on pillars, holding a crucifix and other bright objects, and the effect was of course of inaccessibility, of mystery, of a just-visible inner *sanctum sanctorum,* a place too sacred to be clearly seen or known. It recalled more primitive, or rather, earlier Christianity when it was a mystery cult, a secret society, and a conspiracy, difficult of access, where the privilege to witness parts of the rites had to be won. In the Roman Catholic Church the wall of mystery had been removed, and there was the altar, all of it, in full view, and there were the sacraments, miracles, easily accessible. In the Protestant Churches, for the most part, any suggestion that there might be something mysterious present in church had been completely eliminated, as though there were nothing *unusual* about a Being who lived forever and created the universe, as though a supernatural and eternal God were nothing more than a kind of Bertrand Russell, perfectly understandable if you read the reading list, attended the lectures, and thought.

Somewhere to the right in the blackness a liturgical text was being chanted in singsong, then somewhere to the left. Then the monks in their black robes, some with floor-length black pleated capes, began to glide across the center of the church, voices sailing up and then declining, black batlike shapes drifting across the shiny marble of the floor, incense, chants repeated and repeated, the glitter of candlelight on the Virgin's crown, and at the top of the dome above, Christ Pantocrator; much that was inexplicable, the ceremonial evocation of mystery. God.

The service ended, and we moved into a very small side chapel, perhaps fifteen feet long and ten feet wide, for Mass, sitting in the same kind of high wooden stalls along the left wall. On the iconostasis there was large Madonna and Child to the left of the door, its sweeping silver overlay of drapery gleaming in the candlelight, and a golden halo, the faces and hands alone visible of the underlying painting, dark reddish-brown; to the right of the door, Christ, in the virile, frowning Greek version. Inside the door, in the yellow candlelight, a portly old priest in his celebrant's robes began Mass, chanting in the breaking voice of old age, and two young monks in black in front of us chanted the responses. Now and then the priest came through the doors with the censer, scattering incense and sparks in all directions; it clattered regularly against his robes, making plain why so many monasteries had burned down on Athos.

The two young monks continued their chanting-singing, and gradually, as the time wore on and their chants continued and were repeated and repeated, with the incense filling everyone's head and the candle reflections blurringly shimmering on the holy pictures, slowly and gradually and then more and more strongly fervor entered the Mass, especially the younger of the two young monks was beginning to achieve a state of heightened fervor, to achieve it and to sustain it; that could be heard more and more plainly in his voice, it was there, he was finding it and holding it, and surely we did not exist for him now, and I saw that this high fervor flooding through him must advance and recede from day to day, and month to month, flare and fade, expand and shrink and expand again, and he must be unremittingly in pursuit of it, eight hours a day in church and who knew how many outside.

Suddenly Mount Athos and monasticism itself were transformed. I saw for the first time how a monk's life was possible. It must be built on fervor, and faith, faith in the future, and fervor now. I understood now how someone could spend a lifetime in a monastery, the fervor sustaining his faith. Fervor was the pursuit of joy; the pleasure principle was at work here too, in a monastery. People were one after all. It was joy the young monk sought and found. And he found it because he believed that he was reaching God, and that there was a God to reach. "With faith one can do anything."

There was an inescapable resemblance between him and a drug addict, both with the same obsession to reach and sustain a particular state of euphoria, both neglecting and abusing their bodies, both turning night into day and indifferent to their surroundings, but one going toward horror and the other toward heaven even if heaven didn't exist, toward an interior heaven.

A clock outside struck twelve, Byzantine Time, and daylight began spreading pitilessly through the little chapel, stripping the nighttime magic away from a decrepit old man in an old costume stumbling in and out through a garish wooden partition, and two sallow young men in dusty black singing. The influence of the candles and the icons and the incense turned sour, a spiritual hangover began to throb in the dawn light. But the fervor of the young monk ignored all this, night didn't matter and neither did day, none of that mattered to him any more: he was moving outside time.

We were given breakfast, a crust of bread and a thimble of coffee, then set off along the strange coast toward Vatopédi Monastery. The coast was strange because while it was one of the most fertile stretches of land I had seen in Greece, its atmosphere was one of stunned desolation. Half-timbered shore buildings out of the Middle Ages, balconies sagging on the high face of the mountains, wooden projecting rooms, keeps with a crack like a bolt of lightning rending the ancient stones, watchtowers at the landing stages with empty arrow slits, flying buttresses, bones whitening in the grotto of a church—dead monks were dug up after three years and their bones piled with the others—a thin, streaky waterfall, strange villas gutted by loneliness, a raw unfinished blankness and raggedness, faded, grim, charcoal; the huge foundation of Dionysu Monastery rearing straight up from a cliff, latticy balconies clinging to it, with three stories piling up to a slatternly slate roof, and stark birds tearing wildly around it; Grigoriu Monastery, a white slab on the rocks; Simópetra, high, white and deathly on its cliffs; swatches of old snow in the crevasses of the mountain; old stone villas with wavy slate roofs and decayed loggias, here and there a man, a lay laborer perhaps, idly collecting sticks, or a beggarly old monk sitting; a stillness which now seemed less serene and more threatening, as though Mount Athos in its unworldliness were outward bound toward not heaven but limbo, floating inertly between Athens and Anywhere. An arid aimlessness hung over the coast, and looking upward past the tumultuous hills infested with nature there was the summit of the Holy Mountain, elusive, half-shielded by streaking white clouds.

Vatopédi Monastery presented itself as a vast red-and-white château set on a hillside crowded with trees. It was altogether richer, bigger and neater than Iveron; it had even had electricity for a while, although that had lapsed. The monks took more interest in visitors, and showed us their treasures: an ancient, exquisite mosaic of the Crucifixion; a thousand-year-old Byzantine Imperial Cross; a Ptolemy *Geography;* gorgeous fourth and fifth Century illuminated manuscripts; their most revered icons.

Mount Athos must be the world's greatest treasure house of Byzantine art, not only in its miles of bright, beautiful, and sometimes scaring frescoes, its acres of ancient icons, but also in chalices and crucifixes and all the other furnishings and paraphernalia of the Orthodox faith, donated by all the emperors of Byzantium and the czars of Russia with their famous taste for opulence; and most of all the matchless manuscripts, hand-lettered by masters a thousand or fifteen hundred years ago on parchments of apparently indestructible quality, with their accompanying holy pictures as exquisite and fresh still as an Aegean morning, all gold and blue and red, and shades and degrees: Athos has priceless piles of this lost art.

The monks also described the farms and forests they operated profitably, the crews of lay workmen they employed, giving in all a picture of a fully functioning monastic community with but one flaw, probably fatal: there were only forty-four monks in this community with a capacity of a thousand, which to continue to function needed a vital minimum of a hundred.

One of the three governing Elders took us to a parlor high over the sea for *raki* and Turkish coffee and sweets. He was a plump cheery soul, about sixty years old, with a full gray beard and full Mediterranean gestures when he talked. Lightly attached to the room was a very small and slightly sloping marble balcony. Nothing would do but that we all sit out on it for the view. Remembering that nothing could be done without faith, we sat on it until the sky darkened to a strange gray-purple and an unnatural apocalyptic storm began rolling over the mountains toward us, its clouds full of wild streaks of lightning. We went inside; the clouds burst, and a completely unseasonal summer storm began scourging the mountains.

In the snug little parlor around a kerosene lamp the Elder readily recounted the problems of his religion. How many of the pious, fraudulent beliefs of the people could safely be exposed without damaging their faith? Should they be told that a sacred icon did not really sail all alone from Cyprus accompanied only by a candle? Or that a veil had not really belonged to the Virgin? If all the legends were exposed, he said in passing, "I don't know what would be left." So shifting were the sands of the Orthodox faith and of all Christianity, he felt, that only a union of all Christian sects could save them. "It would have been impossible before," he added, "the people would not have permitted it. But now it is the time; it is possible, because the people are indifferent."

And then he said, "We are very worried here on the Holy Mountain because we are so few, and perhaps before very long there will not be anyone. We are very worried, because if God leaves, He must be found again, and of course He will be found again, but by then, perhaps it will be too late."

God had left Delos because of neglect and now would perhaps leave Athos because of neglect. To go where then?

People have always explained the world in terms of a God, and soon here, of all places, God might be homeless.

And America? Thinking about America, I saw that we would be no help at all, we Americans.

After this long detour into Byzantium, we sailed south again back into the center of the Cyclades and to the famous place just across a generally rough-water strait from Delos, the island of Mykonos.

The island was large and much visited, with fine beaches, two small, modern hotels, a number of restaurants and shops, white windmills with their sails spinning in the wind, and very white streets. The *meltemi* howled without interruption for five days in the bright sunshine. It badgered us whenever we stepped outside, blustering around every step, hurrying us, blocking us, cadging, caroming, shoving, chivying, wind like a pestilential child, ceaselessly nagging you from every side and angle, tireless, insistent, shrill, endlessly inventive but at the same time intolerably monotonous.

However you were free from it within the town. The narrow, turning little streets blocked it off, and as you moved into them and made the first turn this impossible wind was cut off, and you entered into a calm suspension. The labyrinthine streets in the island towns seemed very disorderly and confusing at first, but they had their own logic, adapting themselves to the contours of the land and the chances of ownership, so that houses interwove and overhung and leaned on each other very much in the way a group of young Greeks will hang and lean on and entangle themselves with each other, or the way an island storekeeper will put his merchandise as it arrives down anywhere, so that it is built up in strata like a very old city, the tubes of toothpaste being under a sack of grain, which is under a pile of dresses which are under some lampshades, and he must pick his labyrinthine way by instinct or by memory to excavate a sale.

Petras the Pelican normally sat near the center of the port. His feathers were very beautiful, a pale pink, and he often attended to them with his long narrow bill; otherwise he sat contentedly on the cobblestones near the water. Five years before, a Mykonot fisherman found him, a very young bird, helplessly floating in the sea, having been blown far from home by a storm. Brought back to Mykonos, Petras adjusted to his environment. A local storekeeper told me matter-of-factly what happened then: "He came here and he became very happy, everybody like him, he invited everywhere. He understand hospitality and be polite and he become very popular.

"And so an American man come here, the mayor of Louisiana, and he say, 'I send Petras a woman' and so he send an American girl pelican from Louisiana to Mykonos, but their happiness only be for one month. Because a French man was here making a film, and he feel sorry for Petras too with no woman—the American pelican, her name was Omega, was not here yet—and so he send a French girl pelican. French girls, you know they understand how to seduce, they make appeal, and this French girl pelican, her name is Irenée, she take Petras away from Omega. Sometimes they fight. Petras never fight. He happy all the time, that's why he is so popular. But you, you are going back to America, you will send a man pelican for Omega?"

The curving, sandy beach was sheltered from the *meltemi*. The sea in front of it was bright green for a while, and further out became grape-blue. The water was much more buoyant than in the ocean and as clear as outer space. When kicked, it frothed like champagne. It was always exhilaratingly cool, and never cold. It was so clean that it looked and felt as though no one had ever touched it before.

On the fifth day, Tenos, the next island, emerged from its mist, which meant that the *meltemi* was over, for a while. We hurriedly sailed for Siphnos, and as we came up to it, found another gray, forbidding place, cut off behind its high, desolate natural ramparts. We sailed into a cove enclosed by high bare hills. There was a wharf there and a few houses. We managed to call for the two taxis of the island, and set off in them rattling and shaking up a rocky, unprotected road along the edge of a deep ravine, up through a rugged semiarid landscape like so much of the Mediterranean coastline, and Siphnos seemed another poor, bare Greek island until we reached the top of the climb and saw a very beautiful green upland rolling before us, a highland soft with trees and fields, and a white chain of villages strung along the brow of the hills. There was a feeling of repose everywhere, a feeling that this hidden upland was indeed timeless as most of Greece was not, that there was not layer on layer of past life accumulated here, but instead there was still what there had always been, these houses, these stairways, these trees and flowers themselves, and this abundant feeling of peace. The stillness of the island had penetrated deep into everything and everyone; Siphnos shimmered in the morning light as we walked through all the whiteness of the streets with the brimming green fields next to them.

There were several villages, but they flowed into each other, and it was hard to see where or why one ended and another began. Two of them had names that suited them: Apollonia and Artemóna, named of course for Apollo and Artemis, the son and daughter of Zeus.

A few light blue domes seemed to float on top of these long white villages; here and there were large, ornate white dovecotes; palm trees fanned out amid the many slim cypresses and long-needle pines; and there were small tamarisk trees everywhere, with their knobby trunks and feathery, fernlike leaves; and many grape arbors filtered the strong sunlight into an underwater insubstantiality. Up a stone street-stairway each cobble underfoot was outlined with whitewash; the two or three steps into the houses on both sides were whitewashed; in the tiny terraces of the houses a basin had been excavated in the stone and a drain carved out; on the houses drainpipes to catch the rainwater and lead it into the cistern ran vaguely along the walls, a part of the house's structure; the roofs were flat and whitewashed to catch the rain; in this arctic whiteness a bright orange crowd of oleander spilled out over a wall; a bush heavy with purple blossoms looked like a pile of jewels in a white corner. There were not many people to be seen; a quietness enveloped the long chain of villages passing over the green hills. All the dimensions of the houses were smoothed and rounded; a very small unguarded white stairway went up the side of a more or less Romanesque white church. All the buildings looked as though rich milk had been poured over them and frozen so that no line was very clear any more, the houses and their parts flowed into each other; a wall became a drain became a basin became a step became a wall. All dimensions were blurred, and all designs were the simplest possible. Everything was small, spotless, and done with a deep instinct for natural and man-made beauty flowing together. I had never seen anything like Siphnos before.

At night under the clear Greek moon and the sky of stars, these streets acquired a magical phosphorescence; the silent eerie glow of them all around you gave a feeling as you walked along that you might be about to change into a ram, or a god, and that all the strangest myths of Greece were true.

Raw Kalymnos, island of sponge fishermen, reared like a jagged accident out of the sea. It looked strange and cheerless and doomed, appropriate as the home of sponge fishermen.

They were all away, five hundred of them, off the coast of Africa for six months, diving. Approximately twenty of them would be drowned or maimed, that was known and accepted. In the autumn the fleet of ships would return loaded with sponges, money, and men with banked-up energy to burn. Then Kalymnos springs to life, then the bottles break out, the *tavernas* tremble, the police force enormously increases, and all Greek hell breaks loose.

But now the people of Kalymnos, male-less except for the young up to late adolescence, the old, and the maimed, sat in reverie of their gray, barren, steep rock, in their weird, electric blue, cube-shaped houses, which glowed in peculiar rows up the steep mountainside, waiting for the ships to come in.

Meanwhile we had come in, and a delegation of four young men in their middle teens felt called on to do the honors in the absence of adults. They came to the *Toscana* and issued a formal invitation to tour the town that afternoon at six.

At the appointed hour they arrived, considerably spruced up. Earlier they had been wearing the nondescript slacks and vaguely unbuttoned street shirts, not rigorously clean, which Greek men often wear just to wear something.

Off we went with them at the leisurely Greek pace, which is very important for the visitor to master in the summer, a slow, even stately pace, with a good deal of relaxed arm-swinging and a shifting of weight from hip to hip. It can take a remarkably long time to get anywhere on foot in Greece, but when you do at last arrive you are not panting and sweating from the heat.

"And that is the post office," they said, "and that is our new bus station, and that is a new building there, too, for the market, and there is a very big and important building, a store house."

"They always show us what we already know about," observed Louise Pulitzer, looking longingly back at an elaborate, dilapidated Turkish town house which we had been shepherded past without comment.

". . . and that is the electrical plant . . ."

We were passing an abandoned hall of some kind, with an odd and fascinating oriental facade. "Was that a theater?" asked Louise.

"That? Oh, perhaps. Not used for anything. Now we come to where the taxis wait." And the tour continued on its out-of-phase double track.

Coming back to the quay and the *Toscana* again, in the semidarkness we saw a small fire suddenly break out in a street above us, and I stopped in my tracks as a little girl threw herself across the flames.

"That?" said one of our guides, named Harralambos. "It's some old custom."

Other small children were hurling themselves over the licking flames.

"It's something for the little children," he went on. "Even I," an apologetic chuckle, "did it when I was little."

Little children jumping over fire? What did it mean?

"Old custom. I don't know. For throwing the stone in the sea."

What stone? What sea?

"The stone from the fire," he said.

How did the stone come to be in the fire?

He saw that he was going to have to go into it.

"First you put a stone in the fire, then you jump over the fire three times, and then the next day you take the stone and throw it in the sea, and then we all walk together into the sea. Even the women. With all their clothes on! An old custom."

Other fires were suddenly blazing up in the streets tiered above us, throwing scarlet lights against the bright blue walls, and the shadow of the fire-jumpers flashing along them.

All around us in the steep natural bowl of Kalymnos harbor the flares of fire were breaking out one after another, and there was a feeling of something primordial, of something ritualistic and archaic that was happening to the town.

What did it mean? There were several theories: that jumping over fire was a world symbol of sex fertility, that it was a general rite of purification which had always been associated with Apollo in classical Greece and had survived into Christianity. The day was June 23, the Feast of St. John. As far as the Kalymnians were concerned they were celebrating the Feast of St. John as they had always celebrated it.

On the street ahead of us, three fires broke out. An old woman tossed some kerosene on them, although they had already looked big enough to me. They billowed up higher, and over and through the flames everyone young and old began to jump. A young mother passed her infant back and forth over the fire, and the baby did not cry. "Bravo, darling," the mother whispered happily.

As we watched entranced, our guides began to realize that

we were not going to be satisfied with the post office and the electrical plant, that seeing the new taxi stand was not enough, and that it seemed to be this weary old custom of theirs which commanded all our attention. Very well; they had hoped to keep anything as old-fashioned as that in the background but, very well, if that was what the foreigners wanted. Over the fire with them!

"Come to my house at ten o'clock," said Harralambos. "We will have the celebration."

His house was small and blue, and we sat in chairs on the cement outside the door. His fat mother sat in the doorway, looking pleased and ashamed. Harralambos gave each of the women in our party one flower, and then he served the only refreshments he had to serve: almonds. He had a big bag of them, and at the end of the evening he absolutely insisted that we take the many remaining almonds with us.

From a neighbor a little phonograph was borrowed and it began to play the folk music of Greece, and the young men began to dance, while in the shadows past our circle of light figures crept slowly closer, mostly children but also a lot of women. Soon they were hanging on the low wall just next to us, and filling the balconies of the houses around, and in the trees, and everywhere. Harralambos suddenly shot across and slapped one of them hard, and the crowd fell back, back away from the light and the music and the foreigners which drew them, fell back like a flock clearing out of the way of a wolf; but soon the wolf was back dancing again and the crowd flowed back as close as it could get. They hung there reflecting and commenting on all that we did, a Greek chorus, reacting and laughing and looking puzzled and applauding; Harralambos was persuaded not to slap them again, not to take a switch to the children's bare legs, in other words not to take the normal Greek male's disciplinary measures against the intrusion of children, and the phonograph, the eating of almonds, and the presence of foreigners continued to lift this crowd higher and higher in excitement. Then Harralambos' mother heaved herself out of her chair and led the way to the vacant square of ground next to the house. Here were three large piles of straw and wood shavings in a row. She lit them, tossed a huge splash of kerosene on them, and three sheets of yellow flame shot upward in the darkness. Harralambos turned to me. "You go first."

"Me?"

"Go, go! While the flames are high!"

Obviously fearing I would miss out on the chief pleasure he had to offer, he more or less shoved me at the fire. Seeing nothing else to do, I plunged through or maybe over the flames; a curtain of heat hit the front of my body, and then I was heading for the second fire, jumped through another burning curtain, wondering whether I still had eyelashes and if my pants were smoldering, and on through the third hot sheet. Then I stopped. Nothing seemed to be burned. One after another the Americans came bounding across the flames, wildly cheered at each jump by the crowd, and after them came the people of Kalymnos, the boys and children and the old women, enjoying it more when Harralambos' mother flung more kerosene and higher sheets flared up, throwing vast haunted shadows against the unreal blue walls enclosing us, and hanging smoke on the still night air. In the uproar of the shrieking crowd racing through the smoke and flame, it seemed that they were freeing themselves from something, proving something and shaking loose from some fear.

Afterward they retrieved the pebbles they had thrown in the fire, and the next morning they threw them into the sea, the sea which killed and wrecked for life a sizable number of them every year: they stoned that sea. And then they waded out into it; the sea also gave them the means to live.

Harralambos had two sisters, one more beautiful than the

other. They were about sixteen and eighteen years old; one was fair with dark wavy hair, a beautiful figure and a forthright, laughing attitude, despite the Greek requirement that as a girl she somewhat efface herself in public. The other was darkish blonde, and looked like a goddess of classical Greece. Both had slightly almond-shaped dark eyes, and self-contained, content expressions. You would have thought two such girls would have been the result of generations of carefully nurtured life with all of the advantages, flowers from the hothouse.

Here was their house, two concrete-floored rooms for four people. It had electricity but no other twentieth century convenience. The girls were barefoot; both wore the simplest cotton dresses. Their environment was virtually outside what we in the West think of as civilization; it was a world of donkeys, cobbled streets, bare rock, bare-handed toil, simple to primitive everywhere. Not, however, in the training of the mind. Harralambos was qualified for and going to attend engineering school in Athens the following year. Both the girls spoke competent English and read a lot and knew a lot.

Barefoot in Kalymnos, they carried in themselves the paradox of all Greece: civilization at the bottom of the economic ladder, flowers in aridity, people marked still by the marvel of the classical Greeks but barefoot, the vestiges of a past greater than any other all around them but in ruins, studious and complicated minds but unemployed, beautiful, but in rags, full of vitality, but trapped in the idleness of no opportunity. That was Greece.

We sailed the next day, back through the Cyclades, back across the Aegean to where the first sight of the mainland of Greece appears. This was Sunion, where the Temple of Neptune still faced the sea from its noble, ultimate headland, and where the sun happened to be setting with fantastic beauty and drama, and where someone said that life in the

Aegean islands was certainly very hard but that it was lived, and lived naturally and in its own terms, fully, unlike so many lives in parts of the world where life was easy, and that on the whole and in spite of the incessant hardships of poverty, the islanders had what counted most, a full life lived naturally.

Part

ROME NICE
ANTIBES PARIS
LONDON NEW YORK

Five

The plane rose steeply above Athens, passed quickly above the clouds, shot across the Adriatic Sea to the coast of Italy, went into the long, moaning glide of jet aircraft, and landed at Fiumicino Airport, outside Rome. An American friend met me there with a car, and we drove to a country restaurant nearby, had lunch, and then drove back to the airport. I got into another jet. It lifted steeply above Rome, nosed above the clouds, shot out over the Mediterranean, the stewardess gave me coffee, I drank it, the plane went into the long glide of jets and landed amid the flowers of Nice.

I had a couple of hours before my next plane, and so I took a little bus from the airport along the coast the few miles to Antibes. I had lived there once, and seeing it again was like being slapped by a beautiful woman: every tree mocked me for not knowing enough about how to live, for evasions of the splendor life should have had there; every wall and house told me that I was a fool, forever forgetting what really mattered in life. So I immediately took another little bus back toward the airport, past a Mediterranean that I had never seen so beautiful. It was a pale electric blue, glowing and unreal in such a way that boats on it seemed isolated and bewitched, in the grip of some unnatural sea spell, out there on this phosphorescent slate of blue. Behind the washed coast towns the snow-hung mountains were projected into space, floating in the air, like fortresses about to grind forward toward the cold blue flame of the sea.

I couldn't tolerate it, it represented all the vast possibilities of life that can't be lived, so I went inside and sat in the neutral airport waiting room, out of sight of the South of France. I never expected to see it again.

By the time the plane took off, darkness was falling. Nice and the lights along the coast smoldered and swayed in the darkness, ruby and green and blue and gold, the Riviera from the air looked like a vast cinder bed strewn with the huge, incinerated wardrobe of some distinguished courtesan, bits of her jewelry and satin and sequins and silk, richly colored shreds and points of color scattered everywhere like singed trinkets in a field of ashes.

We landed in Paris, and a French friend met me and drove me to his home. He and his wife and I went to dinner in a houseboat a friend of theirs lives in, moored to the bank of the Seine at the Bois de Bologne. The famous young Frenchman was there. "Well, how was the Arab world? You were bored, true?"

"Yes. No."

"You were bored, you are American, you are always conscious of time, of each passing quarter hour, and in the Arab world they don't know about time, don't care about it. They wait. You other Americans don't know how to wait, that's why you are great and why you are lonely. You don't wait."

"No."

"Life gets by you because of that. You sometimes miss what really matters in life."

"Yes."

"Well, well, gloomy subject for conversation. Excuse me! Now. You went elsewhere."

"To Greece. It wasn't very different as far as time is concerned. They're not very good at it either." I described Mount Athos, its vast edifice resting on faith alone, faith which dwindles a little more every year. I told him what the monk had said, that with faith you could do anything, and without it nothing, and that I was coming to think that he was right, and that at this particular time people had hardly any faith in anything.

He sat frowning silently at his hands.

"Gloomy subject for conversation," I said. "Excuse me!"

"Yes," he said.

The jet rose quickly above Paris, I looked out the window and saw the Channel coast of France going by, and almost immediately the plane started its long glide. As we came over London great clouds hung separately in the sky, their tops bright in the sun, their undersides murky; huge shafts of misty sunshine spread down to the great gray strange city below, which looked to my Levant-conditioned eyes like some ageless Northern lair, thick with mystery and meditation, huddled around great glowing Northern hearths, a place that seemed inhabited only by mystics, and passionate poets, and murderers.

That was how I traveled from Athens to London, a thousand years of civilization's march shot across like that: Athens to London. Here in this gray mystical Northern metropolis the Parthenon metopes were in exile from the unending Greek sky I had just left, all their clarity, realism, nobility and candor, here, embodying here their great message of the splendor and vulnerability of complex man confronting barbarism. And in the end the North—not London particularly but all of the North—needed to be told.

At London Airport I waited for a while, and then the American jet for New York was ready.

As soon as I stepped into the plane America grabbed me, good and bad, left and right. The public-address system was playing a richly arranged, casually swingy version of "Georgia on My Mind." Indirect lighting glowed in big circles over the aisle and in long narrow strips along the walls. Everyone was bigger and busier and better fed than people I had seen for a long time. The atmosphere of a party had been successfully created, and the whole huge tunnel of the cabin seemed spacious and light-filled and busy and confident.

This convention hall took off, passed relentlessly over the Atlantic Ocean, and came down in the morning at Idlewild Airport, which looked like the 1964 World's Fair. At the passport desk the official looked at my green American passport, then up at me, and said in a kind of friendly way, "Welcome home."

America, especially the part of it I knew, was always changing, and I had changed, more than I realized.

The country looked impregnable to me now, a monolith of totally unassailable solidity. It wasn't just that the bridges of New York City seemed made by and for giants, or that a building with a capacity of a town squatted as though forever on a corner I recalled as occupied by a gasoline station, or that a vast highway now went through the air above Connecticut coast towns. It was everything.

It was the earth-shaking power of the United States exerted on the other side of the world, the country's capacity to reach around the globe and alter the history of the Near East, like a strong man who can lift a great weight without getting the main part of his body under it, *out there* on the periphery.

Next to power the most striking thing was the political

stability of the country. I realized now how maturely the government worked, what a responsible instrument it really was. Perhaps you have to live in Syria to see that. Kennedy had beaten Nixon by 113,000 votes, which was .001 of the population, and no flicker of unrest stirred anywhere in the country. Every last garrison and precinct headquarters accepted this tissue-paper victory without a murmur. You probably have to have lived in Syria to appreciate the political maturity of that.

I saw that American politics had this strength, and also that it was not parasitical, not creeping into every last detail of our lives, every minor business transaction, every enterprise. It may seem to have, with taxes and regulations, but it hadn't really, not with the direct interference and control and dominance I had seen elsewhere.

I saw how efficient and effective we were at work, but also how careless, how approximate things were in America. No one took time to be meticulous, scrupulous, immaculate. "That's about right" was the byword for work and workers, and the symbolic tool was the bulldozer.

When I left, the Negroes had been in the courts; I came back to find them in the streets, furiously demanding "equality now." All that time spent looking at Arabs had altered my vision of races, and for the first time I saw the American Negroes as I believe they really are. I had grown up in West Virginia and absorbed the impression that Negroes were probably inferior people, but that wasn't the point: they were just different beings who lived in their own world. Later my mind recognized the unfairness of discrimination, and I knew that Negroes should be fully equal and have all their rights—which are all *every*body's rights—but my feelings, that pack of steadfast and single-minded animals, were not much affected by all these new thoughts.

Now, back in America after so long, I saw Negroes around me and thought, "My God, they're *Americans!*" This came as quite a revelation to me, followed by the sharp thought that their ancestors had all been here longer than mine had. In nationality the facial expressions are everything; the Negroes all had very American expressions on their faces.

I also realized why as a boy I had seen them as set lower and apart, and as a man had been out of contact with them: I was very much afraid of Negroes. I and white society in West Virginia had humiliated them systematically every day; therefore I subconsciously assumed that they would take a ferocious revenge if they got the chance, just as I felt I would have done after such abuse. Vengeance-filled and boiling with hate, I subconsciously sensed the Negroes smoldering on the other side of the railroad tracks, and to save our skins that was where we had to keep them.

I saw now that the "Negro problem" was a white problem, because it was the white people who had to surmount this deep fear, always an extremely difficult thing to do, while all the Negro had to do was to accept being treated like a fully-accredited human being, than which nothing could be easier, and to forgive, which might take some doing. The Negroes didn't want just equality and their rights and more opportunity, it seemed to me now. Just as I would in their place, they want their color to be irrelevant.

In the end it seemed to me that they would get this, because of the best trait there was in the American character. After living in those many far places, I realized that in this country people tended to say "Yes" to aspirations much more than happened elsewhere. In other countries the "No" was either automatic, because the people were negative from habit, or because there were no resources to enable them to say "Yes." Here life tended to say slowly, thoughtfully, "Y-e-e-s-s" to the aspiring people, especially the young ones, if they asked often enough, and asked for the right thing. They tended to get it. That was another American miracle. We're less selfish, suspicious, and jealous; we're willing to give other people a chance. That is our American word: "yes."

Other and darker thoughts of America ran through my head: of course Americans were not as charming as Greeks, hadn't the Italian grasp of style, nor the emotional tone of the Arabs. Americans all had consciences, often bad, guilty consciences, which was why their intimate lives tended to be so abrupt and disjointed. A very, a grimly, a tragically unpoetic country: poetic people were still dropping all around me like flies for lack of anybody to understand the intangible, the twilight, the amorphous in their souls. Society didn't get their messages, and they were still lapsing into alcoholism and suicide everywhere. Americans still missed the point of beauty, and we still didn't individualize ourselves because we were too modest or too dumb to, and our uneasy compromise clothes showed it. Americans lacked coherent characters, and it seemed that the whole population ought to be forced to read *Candide* until the value of cultivating your own garden sank in. The men were still allowed to be slobs because manliness and obtuseness had been equated; the women were still hoping someone would set limits to their rights and responsibilities. The Great American Blur—in self-understanding, housing, faces, billboards, characters, haircuts, schools, shoes, conversation—continued.

Most of all, the American lonesomeness was still balefully haunting the country, haunting especially young Americans. The bleak specter still stalked their lives, and they were still helplessly and stoically putting up with it. It was almost as concrete a problem as unemployment, and I wondered whether the Republicans or Democrats couldn't sweep the next election if they put a really strong Anti-Loneliness plank in their platform, forgetting urban renewal or reforestation for the time being in favor of attacking this inner blight in American lives.

Still, I was very happy to be home, not for any one or any ten reasons. It was just something in the air, something familiar in the American air.